Music Education at a Crossroads

Realizing the Goal of Music for All

Edited by Janet R. Barrett

Published in partnership with
MENC: The National Association for Music Education

Rowman & Littlefield Education
Lanham • New York • Toronto • Plymouth, UK

Published in partnership with
MENC: The National Association for Music Education

Published in the United States of America
by Rowman & Littlefield Education
A Division of Rowman & Littlefield Publishers, Inc.
A wholly owned subsidary of The Rowman & Littlefield Publishing Group, Inc.
4501 Forbes Boulevard, Suite 200, Lanham, Maryland 20706
www.rowmaneducation.com

Estover Road
Plymouth PL6 7PY
United Kingdom

Library of Congress Cataloging-in-Publication Data

MENC, the National Association for Music Education (U.S.). Centennial congress.
   Music education at a crossroads : realizing the goal of music for all / edited by
Janet R. Barrett.
       p. cm.
   Addresses from the Centennial Congress of MENC, The National Association for
Music Education, held in Orlando, Fla. June 25–28, 2007.
   Includes bibliographical references.
   ISBN 978-1-60709-202-5 (cloth : alk. paper) — ISBN 978-1-60709-203-2 (pbk. :
alk. paper) — ISBN 978-1-60709-204-9 (electronic)
   1. Music—Instruction and study—United States—Congresses. 2. School
music—United States—Congresses. 3. MENC, the National Association for
Music Education (U.S.)—Congresses. I. Barrett, Janet R. II. MENC, the National
Association for Music Education (U.S.) III. Title.
   MT3.U5M46 2009
   780.71'073—dc22   2009004786

∞ ™ The paper used in this publication meets the minimum requirements of
American National Standard for Information Sciences—Permanence of
Paper for Printed Library Materials, ANSI/NISO Z39.48-1992.
Manufactured in the United States of America.

Contents

Foreword: Excerpts from Governor Mike Huckabee's Speech to the Centennial Congress[1]

Mike Huckabee

What an honor it is to be at MENC. I want to congratulate you on the big birthday you're having and that's quite a significant one—100 years. That's a pretty good record for any organization. Congratulations to all of you.

Let me begin by telling you a story that I hope will help you to understand why this is so important, not just for me or for you. This is important for every kid in America. In 1966, an eleven-year-old boy had been begging his parents for an electric guitar. His parents were not wealthy; in fact, they were the opposite of that. They were rather poor, and the prospects of this kid getting an electric guitar were pretty remote. It turned out that his parents made what was for them a remarkable sacrifice and ordered from the J. C. Penney catalog an electric guitar that included the guitar, a little amplifier, a music book, and a little gig case. All this for $99. They couldn't pay for it at one time, so they made payments on it over the course of a year.

For Christmas 1966, that little guy got the guitar. He was the most excited kid you can imagine. This was right in the height of the birth and explosion of rock and roll, and this little guy thought that maybe one day he could be a rock and roll star. He took that guitar and he played it for hours and hours on end, to the point that his fingers would bleed, until the calluses had formed, and he continued to play, forming bands in junior high and later in high school, and still continued to play. And many of you

---

1. Arkansas Governor Mike Huckabee served as chair of the Education Commission of the States from 2004 to 2006, focusing on "The Arts: A Lifetime of Learning." Governor Huckabee addressed the Centennial Congress in Orlando, Florida, on June 26, 2007.

are saying, "Oh, I know where this is going. You're going to tell us about a Grammy Award winning musician, somebody who is now at the top of his profession, who all started with that J. C. Penney mail order guitar, paid off over a year." Well no, that's really not the story.

The story is that kid did love to play, and he did continue to play, but he wasn't that good. In fact, he had to find other ways to make a living, like so many musicians do. And he did. He ended up doing things that were quite different than music in many ways, but he never, ever let go of his musical instruments completely. And he's still playing today; in fact he has his own band. You probably have never heard their records. They've not made many television appearances but they ought to. The band is called Capitol Offense and I'm the bass player in that band and I was that eleven-year-old boy back in Hope, Arkansas, who got that guitar, and for me it was life changing. Because it was far more than playing the guitar, it was learning discipline, it was learning teamwork, it was learning how to learn. It was learning that for every minute you have on the public stage, there are endless hours behind the scenes of rehearsal and preparation. And I don't care whatever a person ever learns in life, if you don't learn that important lesson, it's unlikely that one will be very successful.

Today if you ask any CEO of a company what are you looking for in the people you want to bring to your company to make it successful, they'll say, "We need people who understand teamwork, we need people who are disciplined, we need people who are innovative and creative. We need people who understand how difficult it is to prepare for the big picture." And you want to say to them, "You know what you need? You need musicians. That's what you need." Today in America when I hear people talk about how to fix the education system, I think that one of the most obvious things to do is what we're doing the opposite of. At a time when we desperately need a greater emphasis on music and art programs, many districts are stupidly cutting them out of their budgets and giving students the short shrift. Nothing could be dumber to help our next generation of young students more likely fail than to remove from them the capacity of both their left and right brains to function.

Think about what we're doing. Education is not merely the download of data from one brain to the next. Education is ultimately the stimulation of making sure that the inner quest of knowledge is so on fire that the teacher is not standing behind students prodding them, but rather holding them back because they're just so excited about what they're learning that it's a matter of channeling the energy. Now wouldn't that be great if every kid sitting in a classroom today was on fire about learning? Instead, every sixty seconds in this country, two kids drop out of school. We now have a dropout rate of about 30 percent. And as bad as it is to talk about the dropout rate and the fact that two kids every sixty seconds are leaving school, you know what's just as devastating? There are millions of kids sitting in classrooms every day in America taking the most expensive nap in this country as billions of dollars of taxpayer money are being spent so a kid can put his head on his desk and literally sleep through class. One of the reasons that this is happening is not because those kids are dumb. They're just bored. And in many cases they're bored because we have not touched their talent. We are leaving a lot of kids behind because we've created a curriculum that is so narrow, so restricted that we're really not involving all that makes that student a unique human being.

If we take music and art programs from students, it's about more than just taking the aesthetic value of music and art from them. And that alone is tragic. But it is literally sucking the life and energy out of students who desperately need something to touch their creative juices. Great education is not simply the transfer of data. A computer that is nothing more than a database is not very efficient or effective as a computer. But a computer that has a great processor, that knows what to do with the data, can be extremely valuable. It is the music programs of our schools, the art programs of our schools that serve as the processor for our kids—to give them the capacity not simply to know things, but to know what to do with the things they've learned. To give them the chance to be innovative and creative. That's why music programs in our schools are not expendable; they're not extracurricular; they're not extraneous. They're essential. And today, if we're truly serious about changing the nature of education and bringing a whole new generation of creative people into a world in which the future economy is in fact a creative economy, not just a technological economy, not a manufacturing economy, not just a monetary economy, but a creative economy, then the one thing we cannot afford to do is to lose music and art programs.

I want to talk today about unleashing what I call weapons of mass instruction. By the way, these are weapons that we've actually found. In many cases these weapons are sitting in people's attics and under their beds and in their closets, but we need to have these weapons of mass instruction placed into the hands of every child in America. And if we do, I think it's not only changing our education system for the better, I believe it's changing our country for a new level of prosperity and creativity. These weapons have great power. We hear the language of No Child Left Behind, and I appreciate that, but we're leaving children behind if we don't touch the talent of every child. We need to make sure that our ultimate goal is to build in students a life skill that they can live with for as long as they live, not just a school skill that only has value so long as they are enrolled in a school, in a classroom. There is nothing that can go with them throughout their entire journey of life quite as effectively as the study of music. The purpose of these weapons is really so that we build in the next generation, those for whom we are training to be our replacements, true life skills. Music is a lifetime benefit.

Let's talk about what it takes in terms of personnel to operate these weapons of mass instruction. First of all, it takes parents who get behind this at the community level because I think most of us here have as our goal to make sure that music education is accessible to every kid in America. Every kid. It starts with parents. Ninety percent of the parents in America believe that music and art programs should be a part of their child's curriculum and that same 90 percent oppose any cuts in music and arts programs. Give a politician that kind of number and you may just win somebody over. Secondly, proprietors. The people who manufacture and who then provide musical instruments to kids all over the country are certainly passionately interested in making sure that kids have access to music programs in every school. Let me also mention the players themselves. There are millions of musicians in this country, some of whom play professionally. Most of us just play recreationally. But imagine the unleashed power of everyone who has ever been a player. Then add to that the policy groups. There are many, many organizations that are part of a vast coalition pulling together to make sure that this message gets out to the rest of the country. And finally let me mention another group with whom I'm fairly familiar—the politicians. And I don't want you to ignore this group because many of them have simply never taken up the cause because no one's ever asked them. And maybe no one's ever explained it to them.

I'm here today to say these weapons of mass instruction are of little value unless we actually place them in the hands of students all across this country. It would be my goal, my hope, my desire that every student in every school in every school district in this entire country would have a music and an art education at every grade level from a certified teacher from K–12. Anything less than that and we have not yet achieved our goal. That has to be our goal. We passed that kind of legislation in Arkansas during my tenure as governor. I remember the fight. There were people who said "we can't afford it." We argued that we couldn't afford to not have it. There were those who said, "we don't have the teachers." We said, we'll get them. In four years, when it's fully implemented and they have to have all of these courses, we're going to go out to high schools and say, "if you want to be a music teacher, we're going to have a great big job opening in four years for some of you and so you'd better get ready." And you know what happened? Kids went to college to get their music education degree so they could take those jobs. Four years later, when there were some in the legislature who wanted to throttle back our mandates on music and art education for every kid? And, by the way, music *and* art, not music *or* art education. Music *and* art education, every kid, every grade level, certified teachers. And when some of them tried to throttle back, guess who our greatest force was to keep it from happening? All those kids who had just spent four years in college descended on the state capitol and said, "What? Four years ago you guys told us we were going to have opportunities to work in the field, now you're talking about scaling it back? I don't think so!" And that just nailed it.

We need, first of all, a plan to implement and deploy the weapons. Let me quickly make some suggestions. First, the state and local level is the place where it will happen. There has always been sort of a sense that if we can get the national and the federal government to get excited, we're going to win. No, let me suggest that the best way to win this is through battlefields at a time at the state and local level. One of the reasons is because education policy is really not driven by Washington; it's driven by the states. And secondly because it is easier to get things accomplished at a state level than it is at the federal level. Innovations happen at a state and local level. It's a much more manageable playing field. Plus, as innovations are made at state and local levels, things that are really brilliant that work will be shared with other states. Things that don't work won't be repeated as a mistake in all fifty states. Make the focus state level with local support.

Secondly, never forget that in government, you only fund what you force. If you don't force it, you don't fund it. The goal is not so much to talk about the money that you need, the goal is to get built into the law mandates that force the issue. If you force the issue, then you have to fund it. If you just talk about the funding, then you're going to be fighting on the wrong battlefield. Force the issue of implementation of mandated curriculum for music and art programs. That's got to be the goal, and let the funding be the issue that you deal with only as you are getting to the reality of the mandated programs.

The third rule is this: You only improve the games in which you keep score. Think about this. How many people get really excited about a PE dodge ball game? Why not? Because we don't keep score and nobody cares. What we get excited about are the high school basketball teams and the football teams, because they have scores and there's a win/loss record. So what we need to do is find ways in which we can keep score and build community pride. There are a number of ways to do it, some of which are the obvious—band competitions, choir competitions, things at which we excel. But there are other ways to keep score and one of the challenges we have in terms of implementing the curriculum is that a lot of politicians aren't really worried, and a lot of school boards and school superintendents don't get excited about music and art programs because we don't have as effective a way to score their value. I want to be careful that we don't get so test-focused in music and art that we test the creativity out of the kids. That's not the goal. But Kentucky and Oklahoma are a couple of the states that are experimenting with ways of having a measurement system or an evaluation system that tests the value or efficacy of the programs. That's important because what we keep score on, we consider to be important.

We need to expand the reach. Make sure there are more people involved. In Arkansas we started a program called "Play It Again, Arkansas." It's a simple program, and other states have adopted it. We asked people all over our state to donate musical instruments they weren't using, instruments that were sitting in their closets or under their beds and their attics. Music stores across our state willingly donated their services to rehabilitate those instruments and get them in first-class condition because there's nothing worse than handing a kid an instrument that's not worth playing. That's a discouragement to a child; it's not what we want to do.

So we got those instruments in great shape and if they weren't repairable, we didn't use them. We had thousands of instruments donated and for kids whose parents couldn't afford to buy or even to rent instruments, we were able to put in their hands everything from trumpets to drumsticks to tubas to bassoons—you name it. Every kind of instrument started showing up. We gave the donors a nice tax deduction for the gift. Then we gave those instruments to band directors all over the state who put them in kids' hands. And it was amazing how many kids were able to play. I'll never forget standing at the All-State band competition listening and having a band director pull me aside and point out a kid who was first chair and say, "I just want you to know that kid a year and a half ago got an instrument from Play It Again. His parents couldn't afford it and now he's working his heart out, and he's first chair in the All-State Band." And I thought, here's a kid that may get a college scholarship because somebody put in his hands a weapon of mass instruction.

Another key issue is to build a bipartisan team. Approach the governor of your state, key legislators on both sides of the House and Senate, and then bring to bear spheres of influence—the arts community, and arts councils in most cities and counties. If you don't have a personal relationship with the governor of your state, find out who does and keep finding out who does until you find someone that you discover is already passionate about music, or you could lead him or her to be. You've got to get into the first level and that is making the governor aware of how important this could be. Secondly, make contact with some of the key legislative leaders. Get those Democrats and Republicans. This is not a horizontal issue. This is not about left and right, liberal and conservative, Democratic and Republican. This is a vertical issue—we're either up or we're down. We're either going forward or we're going backwards. What we need to be able to do is to show people that this is beyond the politics that divide most of us. This is a unifying issue. Nobody owns it, except the people who can see the value of making sure that every kid gets a chance to touch his or her creative self. Get those folks together—the key senators, key legislators. Like any other organization, start with the ones that you can get to go with you. Then you get them sold on it, and get them to sell some of their colleagues on it. You just keep selling it until you have enough votes.

We used to say in committee meetings, you don't need to have everybody in agreement. If there's a committee of eleven people, you only have to count six. Politics is really a simple game of math. It's a matter of getting enough votes until your side passes something and wins it. It's really not as difficult as some people would make it seem. It seems like this monolithic, unattainable goal. I'm telling you—if a state like Arkansas that has historically been seen as an impoverished and underfunded state can mandate music and art programs for every kid in every grade taught by certified teachers, there's no excuse for any state in the country not being able to say we can do that, too, and even do more. That's why we have to move forward with it.

The net result is that we raise up a whole new generation of people who understand what music can do for them. I would not be standing here talking to you today had it not been for the discipline and the confidence of getting up in front of people that I did not know. I didn't have it because I grew up in a household where we didn't have a lot, and I grew up in a household where I always felt I wasn't quite as good as the other kids. I'm the first male in my entire family who ever graduated from high school. My parents wanted me not only to finish high school, but to go on to college. They wanted me to have a life that was better than the one they had. As I look back, the reason that I know they made the sacrifice to pay out an electric guitar over a year is that they thought maybe this is his ticket. Maybe this is what's going to help him break out of the poverty and have a start at what we didn't have.

And so whatever the reasons, this shy, bashful little kid who played that guitar to the point that his fingers nearly bled, finally got up enough courage to get up in front of people to play, because playing became more important than the fear of being on the stage. I wonder how many kids out there in America are kids just like me? Just like millions of others and maybe just like you for whom music, somehow, unlocked your inner self and your potential. And today, maybe you're a music teacher because somebody invested in you and you look at your life as an opportunity to invest back in others. However that may be, I hope you'll realize that the chances are great that we could take on a whole new world and win a war if we unleash the weapons of mass instruction. Thank you. It was a pleasure to be with you.

Introduction: Realizing the Goal of Universal Music Education

Addresses from the Centennial Congress of MENC— The National Association for Music Education

Janet R. Barrett

It is the right of every child to receive a balanced, comprehensive, sequential music education taught by qualified music teachers. This statement, simple in its construction but profound in its implications, characterizes the central mission of MENC: The National Association for Music Education. From its early history to the present, the leaders of MENC have held strongly to the belief that all students should have access to music instruction as an integral component of school experience. Within that broadly encompassing aim, music educators are called to serve our very youngest children; students with disabilities; students whose lives are affected by poverty; students in rural, urban, and suburban settings; and students who represent the ever-expanding ethnic and racial diversity of American society. Increasingly, music educators have turned their attention to learning beyond the traditional school-age years as well, promoting a lifelong view of musical engagement, and to increasing the range of musical offerings within schools in an effort to engage students who have typically not elected to continue the study of music beyond traditional curricular requirements in elementary grades.

The latter half of the statement speaks to the quality of that musical experience, seeking balance across instructional levels, comprehensiveness in scope both through representative musical styles and genres and in numerous forms of music making and study, and sequential organization to ensure the development of deep and rigorous understanding. It is also highly appropriate that qualified teachers are at the center of realizing this mission, for those teachers constitute the core of MENC's membership. Through its history, the association has been committed to substantive and innovative programs for the preparation and professional development of teachers; their vital role in shaping students' musical experience is critical in realizing the goal of universal music education.

Throughout MENC's history, we have taken stock of the status of the music education profession at various crucial turning points. These appraisals have been prompted by milestones, such as anniversaries or the turn of a new century, or by pivotal changes in schools and society warranting our critical examination and response. Lilla Belle Pitts, president of MENC from 1942 to 1944 and organizer of MENC's Golden Anniversary Observance in 1957, wrote that the event should have "much deeper significance than just a year-long birthday party" (1956, 23). Many such turning points have been commemorated in statements of advocacy, vision, or focus (see the appendixes of this book for a representative sample). The statements on the value of music study convey unanimity of purpose and provide a core of principles to guide the association's initiatives. These statements embody MENC's historical emphasis on curriculum and the professional development of teachers, while also reflecting more recent emphases on advocacy, policy, and strategic alliances with partners who support music education.

Over the past few decades, The National Association for Music Education has provided professional leadership in crafting position statements that communicate the benefits of music and arts education with clarity and passion. Recent examples include the Housewright Declaration (1999) and the "Value and Quality of Arts Education: A Statement of Principles" (1999), which was signed by ten professional education associations in a widespread show of support. The National Association for Music Education has also worked to build alliances with these associations and policy influencers to establish and maintain well-organized coalitions for music education. In 2005, Congressional Resolution 45 of the 109th Congress identified music as "an important component of a well-rounded academic curriculum [which] should be available to every student in every school." Such proclamations are symbolically meaningful to music teachers, who are often asked to justify the role of music in school communities. We question, however, whether they have been persuasive tools for advocacy and action. In many communities, this inspiring rhetoric of support has unfortunately not always been heeded by policymakers who make decisions that influence the quality of music programs for students and the daily conditions in which music teachers work.

MENC planned several events to commemorate the historic milestone of a century of service to the profession, including a series of events led by the History of Music Education Special Research Interest Group, a conference at Keokuk, Iowa, and celebrations at the Orlando Centennial event. From the outset of planning, however, the National Executive Board (on which I was serving at the time), expressed a strong interest in marking the occasion with an event of significant weight, mirroring the desires of our predecessors a half century earlier. We thought it appropriate to engage those within the profession but also those allies, partners, supporters, and advocates in other associations and representing other entities to join with us in a two-day summit of focused presentations, discussions, and dialogue. An organizing principle was to use the Congress as a venue for bringing together various arenas of practice, policy, research, advocacy, and leadership to address the inherent difficulties in realizing the goal of universal music education for all students. In this spirit, the mission of the Centennial Congress was formed.

MENC leaders were in agreement that the work of this Congress should animate strategic planning, inform advocacy efforts, and strengthen alliances with associations and allies who share our commitment to universal music education. Accordingly, we invited leaders from a wide representation of associations, organizations, and government agencies to help us think strategically and identify new opportunities for action. In seeking the good counsel of those representatives, we acknowledged that the obstacles that stand in the way of widespread access to a quality music education are formidable, significant, and we realize, greater in scope than we are able to address on our own. At the same time, we take full responsibility for building on these insights to direct the future activities and initiatives of our profession.

FOCUSING THE CENTENNIAL CONGRESS

Reaching this milestone of 100 years is a time for celebration; it is also a time to assess and reflect on progress we have made in realizing the values we hold for music education. The purpose of the Centennial Congress was to discuss two key issues, which were distributed to participants as they convened:

- *Our shared goals for music education.* For decades, the broad education community has been in agreement with the music education community on the importance of music for every child in America. We need to review and renew this agreement in light of current trends in education and society.
- *Why, despite our longstanding agreement on goals, music education is not yet universal.* Even without precise data on the status of music education programs around the nation, it seems clear that some large percentage of American children—estimates hover around half of the total population—do not receive a credible music education.

The overriding question discussed during the Congress was: What conditions must be met if we are to reach our shared goals for music education?

TOWARD REALIZING THE GOAL

Over two days, participants in the Congress heard addresses from notable music educators as well as individuals representing school administration, state boards of education, and school board associations. Former governor of Arkansas Mike Huckabee was asked to speak to the Congress on the basis of his term chairing the Educational Commission of the States and his outspoken support of arts education at the state and national level. He described his own musical awakening and the impact of his early participation in music on the course of his public life. Excerpts from Governor Huckabee's speech serve as a foreword to the addresses that follow in this collection. Particularly useful to music educators are his recommendations for building coalitions of support to prompt legislative action.

During the Congress, a small panel attended the breakout sessions in which the participants discussed the challenges of meeting the goal of universal music education as well as topical themes that included curriculum, assessment, music teacher education, collaboration across associations, and organizational planning. The Centennial Declaration, crafted by Paul Lehmann, Bennett Reimer, Michael Mark, and Janet Barrett, with assistance from Michael Blakeslee, was written during the Congress to reflect consensus on the overarching principles to guide programs and policy.

It seemed fitting to ask one of our most accomplished historians in the field, Michael Mark, professor emeritus of Towson University, to speak to the Congress on this occasion. During the varied activities of the yearlong Centennial Celebration, the community of historians within music education has been especially crucial in situating the profession's longstanding desires and goals in historical perspective. Mark provides a sample of this fruitful work in tracing the relevance of music education as seen through three crucial periods of American history—the Industrial Revolution, the Great Immigration that spanned several decades before and after 1900, and the Civil Rights era. Mark reminds us of the powerful notion that society's prevalent challenges and aspirations are reflected in its hopes for public education.

The Centennial Congress was honored to hear from Bennett Reimer and Paul Lehman, whose varied involvements in crafting the National Standards, participating in the Housewright Symposium, the International Policy Symposium, and countless other initiatives brought a depth of perspective and breadth of experience to the discussion. Bennett Reimer, John W. Beattie Professor of Music Education Emeritus of Northwestern University, challenges music educators to analyze how our overall goals for universality have been aligned with our actual practices. He argues persuasively that we must evaluate music programs for their relevance and relation to the various musical roles that are valued by society. Taking Reimer's challenge seriously entails preserving our traditional strengths while branching out into curricular territory that will make the study of music compelling and meaningful to a broader range of students. For the association, Reimer calls for "leadership for both preservation and innovation" in order to revitalize school music programs. As we contemplate future growth and reflect on past successes, Reimer calls the profession to thoughtful analysis and courageous action.

Paul Lehman, professor emeritus of music education of the University of Michigan and past president of MENC (1984–1986), speaks with clarity and passion about six conditions that must be met if music education is to realize its goal of universal music education. He speaks with deep conviction to the importance of the National Standards as a curricular framework that enables a balanced and comprehensive curriculum, and to the pressing realities of convincing educational stakeholders of the essential need for strong music programs. His analogies and examples are clear and compelling. They arise from a breadth of experience that relates big picture issues to specific local concerns. Lehman's address helps to explain why we have not achieved our common goals, while providing common sense principles to guide our best efforts.

The remarks of Samuel Hope, executive director of the National Association of Schools of Music, illuminate why our focused efforts to build widespread support and recognition for music study have not been widely valued and forwarded in policy initiatives. He addresses the frustration of the profession that music is often not afforded the same parity of recognition it deserves as a field of study and achievement. Drawing on his formidable understanding of policy, Hope describes four fundamental areas of recognition, protection, creativity, and strategy that can be appraised and analyzed in moving forward toward greater public acknowledgement of music education. Of particular urgency are six principles Hope enumerates to guide our strategic efforts to enhance public acknowledgement of music education.

Regardless of the influence of federal policies or national professional associations such as MENC, the reality is that most decisions about the scope and structures of American public education are made at state and local levels. Accordingly, we must clarify how policies and processes work in our respective regions and communities. Anne Bryant, executive director of the National School Boards Association, and Brenda Lilienthal Welburn, chief executive officer of the National Association of State Boards of Education, participated in a panel discussion of these arenas for advocacy and political action. Their remarks have been transcribed in order to provide guidance for building stronger agendas that will influence state and local decision making.

As coordinator of the Centennial Congress, I would also like to note the contributions of other speakers, including Paul Houston, executive director of the American Association of School Administrators; Donald A. Hodges, director of the Music Research Institute at the University of North Carolina; and Don Ester, chair of the Society for Music Teacher Education. As MENC president, Lynn Brinckmeyer directed the activities of the National Executive Board and other state and national leaders, who facilitated discussions throughout the event. These discussions provided a forum for participants' responses, and for gathering valuable insights to motivate strategic planning at the state and national level.

In addition to the addresses given at the Congress, we have provided a compendium of various historical documents as appendixes so that readers can trace primary, salient themes across decades of professional activity as well as noting changes in our goals and priorities.

The Centennial Congress raised critical issues at a notable historical turning point in the history of MENC: The National Association for Music Education. Music educators, state and national leaders, and strong allies and advocates for music education must sustain this dialogue and act strategically in realizing the goal of music education for all students.

ACKNOWLEDGMENTS

The editor wishes to thank Michael Blakeslee, Fran Ponick, Sue Barus, and Sean C. Potts for their assistance with this project.

REFERENCES

Pitts, Lilla Belle. "The Golden Anniversary Observance." *Music Educators Journal* 42, no. 4 (1956): 23–26.

1

A Centennial Declaration of MENC: The National Association for Music Education

Michael Mark, Bennett Reimer, Paul Lehman,
Janet R. Barrett, and Michael Blakeslee

We are in agreement that the basic ideals long expressed by the music education profession and other education professionals are still current: *it is the right of every child to receive a balanced, comprehensive, sequential music education taught by qualified music teachers.*

A healthy society requires musically fulfilled people. The primary purpose of education is not to create a workforce; it is to improve the quality of life for individuals and for society. Although music education has been valued throughout history for its unique contributions, it is not yet universal in American schools. Serious problems persist, including inequality of access, uneven quality of programs, and insufficient valuing of music as a part of the curriculum. As a result, music is often pushed to the periphery of the school experience. In this centennial year of 2007, we reaffirm our longstanding ideals in a challenging context that calls for directed action in curriculum, assessment, research, teacher education, advocacy, and building alliances.

NEEDS REGARDING CURRICULUM

Our curriculum must reflect more than our own desires; it must reflect the needs and desires of the students we serve. We seek contexts and modes of instruction that will provide students with more inclusive experiences of the styles and genres of music and the many musical roles that are practiced within our society and that are represented in the national content standards. We need to develop programs that are flexible and of greater variety than those currently in use in most schools. This will require efforts including identifying and promulgating effective models, rethinking teacher education, expanding in-service development opportunities, and developing new assessment techniques. These initiatives necessitate an expansion of our research interests and a greater application of research results in teacher education programs and in classrooms. We need to develop deeper insight into the role of music in general education, focusing on what is distinctive about music and on its complementary relationships to other subjects. We need electives as broad and diverse as the interests and enthusiasms of our students.

NEEDS REGARDING ASSESSMENT

We need assessment techniques and strategies that are suited to the domain of music in all its complexity and diversity. We need to focus our energies on the development of multiple assessment strategies that reflect the dimensions of students' musical growth and draw upon a broad range of instructional methodologies and techniques. We need assessment criteria that go beyond attendance, effort, and attitude. We need formative assessments of students' learning—including portfolios and other techniques, and we need evaluations based on the Opportunity to Learn Standards.

NEEDS REGARDING ADVOCACY

We need to arrive at ways to transmit a uniform message to decision makers and to the public. We need strong alliances with those who share or understand the value of music study and are willing to join with us in advocating for strong, vibrant music programs. We need to make advocacy efforts that clarify and celebrate the enhanced opportunities to learn that we are striving to make available.

TOWARD THE FUTURE

We will build on our first hundred years of success with a second century of leadership and service. Our musical culture, our students, and our society deserve no less.

2

Music Education and National Goals

Michael Mark

We tend to think of the benefits of music education in the context of the individual, the school, or the community, but we often overlook the role that our profession plays in supporting national goals. As we examine the history of American music education, we should view it as an integral part of the history of our nation. I think of American history as a colorful tapestry made of tens of thousands of individual threads woven together. Each thread represents an aspect of our history—economic, political, military, education, and so on. One thread represents music education, and the tapestry would be incomplete without it. Our profession has a place in our national history that we need to recognize and to honor.

It is in this broader context that I will speak about the rationales that supported the introduction of music in American schools as a curricular subject. Then I will talk about the role that music education played during three critical periods in American history.

Music first became a curricular subject in the Boston schools in 1838 after Lowell Mason successfully advocated for it to the Boston School Committee. The committee agreed to include music in the curriculum because it met the three criteria against which all subjects were measured: Was it moral? Was it physical? Was it intellectual? Music was considered moral because of its role in religion, and religious music was not considered inappropriate for schools at that time. In fact, the morality of music instruction went beyond religion. The committee report stated that music produced happiness, contentment, cheerfulness, and tranquility. It was considered beneficial for children physically because singing was good for the lungs, or what the committee report referred to as the "organs of the breast." The intellectual part of the justification was a bit of a stretch. Music was said to contribute to intellectual development mostly because it had been a component of the classical curriculum, the quadrivium, as far back to the Middle Ages, as though that in itself proved the intellectuality of music. The quadrivium consisted of the study of geometry, mathematics, astronomy, and music. As a quadrivial subject, music was actually a mathematical study. It was almost as though the committee was saying that if it was good enough for the professors of the Middle Ages, then it must be good enough for us. On the other hand, the committee sounded quite contemporary when it professed that music contributes to memory, comparison, attention, and intellectual faculties.

The three criteria—intellectual, moral, physical—justified the establishment of music in many school systems as it spread throughout the country during the rest of the nineteenth century. As late as 1895, the British philosopher Herbert Spencer referred to these criteria as the basis for education, and some American writers continued to refer to them in justifying music education programs into the first decade of the twentieth century.

THE INDUSTRIAL REVOLUTION

Now, consider the three critical historic periods of American history. Each had to do with our nation's cultural identity. The first was during the first half of the nineteenth century, the time when music first became a curricular subject. We have to go back earlier in our history, though, to understand how music came to serve national needs in the 1830s. Music education in colonial America was a private entrepreneurial practice in which singing masters wrote their own music and traveled from one location to another to lead classes of adults and children in learning to read music and in singing. The original purpose of the singing schools was to develop musical abilities that would improve the quality of church services. As the singing schools gained in popularity they became social occasions as well. The music of the singing schools was characteristically bold and vital, sometimes beautiful. But the singing masters were not trained composers. Their music violated many of the accepted European principles of composition such as parallel fifths and octaves and other musical crimes that we all learned not to commit in Theory 101. In other words, in comparison with the European music of the time, it was crude and unsophisticated, unrefined by European standards.

The industrial revolution had started in the previous century in England and by the early nineteenth century was taking hold in the United States. By the 1830s, American cities were expanding as the revolution created new employment opportunities. As this was happening, the United States was slowly evolving from an agricultural to a manufacturing and mercantile society. As the middle and upper economic classes grew, they wanted to become consumers of the finer things in life. They recognized that the quality of American culture was far behind that of Europe. They knew this because European musicians traveled here to perform, and many other musicians emigrated here to become music teachers. It was a rich time in the history of European music. Franz Schubert and Robert Schumann were alive, and Beethoven had died only a few years earlier. Those Americans who wanted their country to be an equal among nations believed that our homegrown music had to be replaced with music from across the ocean, or at least with music similar to that of Europe. They came to view the music of New England as archaic, belonging to country people and not appropriate for sophisticated city dwellers.

It was the job of the schools to help shape a cultivated, well-educated populace, and music was one of the tools by which this could be done. From its inception in 1838, the music used in school programs was based on European principles of structure and harmony. This was the beginning of teaching American children to appreciate traditional classical music and the beginning of the end for the old New England music. From that time on, as school music spread throughout the country, more and more American children sang songs that helped guide them toward adulthood in a country whose culture would equal that of Western European countries. In this way, music education helped the United States change its self-identity from a rural nation to an urban, industrialized one.

THE GREAT IMMIGRATION

The period from about 1880 to 1920 brought a new phenomenon to the United States. It had always been a nation of immigrants, but this particular period saw a huge influx of people from eastern and southern Europe. Life had become so difficult in many countries that people could no longer earn a living, or they were persecuted to the point where they had to leave just to survive. The United States, on the other hand, had a burgeoning economy based on its ever-growing industry. The labor unions had gained strength, and wealthy industrialists were eager for a new source of labor that would accept less pay and fewer benefits, if any at all. As difficult and unfair as working conditions were in the United States, many immigrants found life in the New World an improvement over their lives in their native countries.

The influx of millions of immigrants from many countries created new problems for the United States. The newcomers were mostly uneducated, didn't speak English, and dressed, ate, and worshiped differently from the already established Americans. Rather than allowing the newcomers to dilute the national identity with a polyglot of cultures, the new Americans had to be acculturated so they would be more like those who had been here for generations. This was the time of what was called "the melting pot." The phrase came from the title of a play written by a British playwright, Israel Zangwill, who admired the ability of America to absorb so many strangers from such profoundly different backgrounds. A famous line in the play read, "America is God's crucible, the great Melting-Pot where all the races of Europe are melting and reforming!" Zangwill's play became a metaphor for the way that the United States was attempting to make immigrants into Americans. The play was written in 1908 and its centennial comes one year after that of MENC.

There were several areas of society where this cultural transformation could take place—the workplace, the military, the streets, and most of all, the schools. By acculturating the children of immigrants, the schools helped assure that future generations would speak English and would look, act, and even think like other Americans. And the children would help teach their parents to be Americans as well. The role of music educators at that time was to teach national and traditional American songs that would help young people come to appreciate their new country. A review of the music used in schools during that period reveals a strong leaning toward songs that best portrayed America, such songs as "The Star Spangled Banner" (which was not the official national anthem at that time), "America the Beautiful," and Stephen Foster songs, among others.

Music educators went even farther than that. The Music Supervisors National Conference (now MENC), was founded in 1907. Only six years later, MSNC published a song book for community singing, which was a popular activity at that time. The book *Fifteen Songs for Community Sings* contained national and traditional songs for adults and children who took part in community sings across the country. This was MENC's first effort to educate adults beyond the walls of the schools. In a few years the book was expanded to *55 Songs for Community Sings*, and then *Twice 55*, and it served the country well as a unifying force during World War I.

THE CIVIL RIGHTS REVOLUTION

The third historic period was when American laws and hearts finally took up the difficult task of recognizing that all Americans, regardless of race, had equal rights in every area of American life. Later, civil rights came to include gender, disabilities, and other factors, but race was the central issue at first. Schools in many parts of the country had been legally segregated since 1896, when the Supreme Court's *Plessy v. Ferguson* decision decreed that "separate but equal" was constitutional. Separate schools for whites and blacks became the law of the land in many parts of the country. The civil rights era began with the historic 1954 *Brown v. Board of Education of Topeka* Supreme Court decision which desegregated American schools. Although schools could no longer be segregated after the 1954 decision, integration took place very slowly. In fact, many American schools are still not integrated to this day. By the 1960s, Americans were tired of the unfairness of segregation and began to demonstrate for equal civil rights. The landmark Civil Rights Law of 1964 finally guaranteed equal rights for all Americans.

The schools were among the most important institutions for implementation of the civil rights laws, and by the latter part of the 1960s, curricula were beginning to address multicultural issues. Music was a natural component of multicultural education because every culture has its own unique and distinctive music. The Tanglewood Symposium of 1967 was a turning point for multicultural music education because the "Tanglewood Declaration" stated that music of all cultures should be part of the school music program. Shortly after the symposium, music educators began to

expand their horizons to learn about musics beyond those that traditionally had been part of the school program. Leaders of the multicultural music education movement developed, and soon publications and recordings
began to appear to assist music educators in teaching the music of many
cultures. Multiculturalism has been a staple of music education programs
since that time, and millions of students have heard, experienced, and
made music of cultures other than their own. In this way, multicultural
music education became an important part of the process of unifying the
many peoples of the United States.

CONCLUSION

In comparing the role of music education during three historic periods of
American history, it is ironic to note how national goals change. In the
first period, when music was new in schools, it was used to help Americans become more like Europeans. During the next period, the Great
Immigration, music was used to help Europeans become more like Americans. Finally, during the Civil Rights Era, music was used not to change
anybody's identity, but to help students learn to respect, honor, and live
with cultures other than their own. Each of the three periods was critically
important in helping Americans create a national cultural identity that was
right for its time. In each case, music proved to be an important tool in
achieving national goals.

I hope that music educators will come to see how important their work
is to the nation, and will recognize that their profession has played a critical role in the evolution of our democracy through the centuries.

3

The National Association for Music Education: Leadership for What?

Bennett Reimer

The Music Supervisors National Conference, the Music Educators National Conference, the National Association for Music Education; by whichever name we are alive and well at age 100. When the comedian George Burns was approaching that age he said that he had gotten so old that when he went into a restaurant and ordered breakfast, they asked him for a deposit. Yet here is our professional organization in its centennial year, hale and hearty, justifiably proud to have survived the many challenges presented by the educational storms it has encountered during 100 years of turbulence. And it is still providing leadership as it has throughout its history. Impressive and admirable. I am grateful to have been a member for more than half of its history, and to have had the opportunity to contribute in some small way to many of its ambitious leadership initiatives during that time. Those initiatives have influenced me in a variety of important ways, helping to form me as a professional, as they have every member.

Now we face another moment of challenge, as is appropriate in such a significant milestone year. We need to celebrate this birthday and have every right to do so. Yet, I want to propose, all is not well in the profession of music education. If we want to perpetuate its life we need to address the hard realities facing us now, realities that can threaten our well-being in serious ways. As with our love of our nation, our love of our profession requires us to recognize both its strengths and its weaknesses, and to do all we can, honestly and forthrightly, to ameliorate our weaknesses as boldly as necessary in order for us to survive with improved health and heightened influence. We need leadership, at every level from individual members to large-scale cooperative endeavors, to help us preserve the good from our past and our present, and to redefine the good in ways that ensure our continuing relevance in a fast-changing future, especially fast-changing in the fields of music and of education.

Our need for redefinition is captured in a most poignant way in the second issue posed by the charge to the Centennial Congress. "Why," it asks, "in light of our longstanding agreement on goals, is music education not universal?" This question touches us deeply, in its sorrowfulness and its honesty. We have tried so hard, over so long a time, with such dedication, to achieve our goals. Yet we are faced, sadly, with an incontrovertible fact: universality, or "basicness," full acceptance as being equal to the obligatory foundational subjects in schooling, remains as elusive as it has always been. The furthest we have gotten is lip service, the privilege of being listed among the basics in several official-sounding documents, but with little of the support needed to back it up. Cold comfort.

I want to argue that there are two major causes of our historically secondary status in education. The first is at a level largely beyond our control and largely unrelated to the specifics of our work. That level has to do with the underlying value system of our culture, in which success in life is measured primarily by economic criteria. We can be and must be a strong voice to counterbalance that deep-seated conviction with a rationale that stresses the humane, life-enhancing effects of experiences with music and the arts. But we must not mislead ourselves to assume that we can, by our good intentions, turn that battleship in a new direction when so many powerful forces keep it steaming full speed ahead. That particular dimension of the relatively low value from which we suffer requires a long-term perspective, which I must refrain from trying to address here and now.

The second cause of our plight turns attention to ourselves, and directly and precisely to our longstanding agreement on our goals. That, I propose, is what has been the major impediment to our being as universal—as pertinent to the musical interests and needs of everyone in our culture—as it is possible for us to be. Our goals, I argue, have been remarkably narrow, remarkably limited, remarkably unrelated to the musical needs and desires of the great majority of our population. For the small minority that has embraced our predominant goal of achieving musicianship as we have defined it, that is, as being a performer of composed music primarily in large ensembles, we have indeed come very close to success, to being as universally relevant to their particular needs as is likely in an imperfect world. Of that achievement we deserve to be very proud. We have every reason to celebrate it and to continue to be devoted to preserving it and enhancing it in all possible ways.

But our success in that goal is insufficient to establish our universality, our basicness. No matter how hard we try, through as much advocacy as we can engage in, we cannot sell that one aspect of music—necessary and valuable as it is to the few who relate to it—as being our only, or nearly only, contribution to the musical education of our populace; our only or nearly only goal as a profession at the level of what we actually offer in schools beyond the elementary and middle school grades. In those grades, too often, classroom music experiences, in their unauthenticity to the ways music is actually experienced and enjoyed by our students, tend to fade fast from the memories of those who have had them.

The appearance in 1994 of the National Standards for Music Education was the clearest signal we have ever had that our most visible, most dominant goals were focused on just three of the nine aspects of our culture's musical knowings and doings that the standards identified; numbers one and two dealing with performance, along with number five, reading and notating music because those learnings are required for the kinds of performance that we almost exclusively provide for in our programs. No longer could we pretend that we were pursuing two overarching aims that we had historically claimed were essential for our success—comprehensiveness and balance in our program offerings, both in general education in music and specialized education in music. And no longer can we pretend that all the other ways to be musical identified in the content standards can be as well served as they deserve to be through cramming all of them into our existing performance ensemble offerings. Comprehensiveness, in that contrivance, is a sham, and balance goes out the window. As a result, we remain where we always have been, magnificently effective in serving the needs of the few while deplorably ineffectual in serving the needs of everyone else. Universal? A pipe dream.

Now more than ever, as we rightfully celebrate what we have been, we await a liberating ideal of what we can become. That ideal, I devoutly hope, will be one in which we democratize our goals, recognizing that at present, reflecting our past, we provide excellent opportunities to be musical, but only in the one way that we prefer, thereby deciding for everyone how they can be musical, a program more autocratic than democratic. As a result, the majority of people, determined to be musical and finding our offerings unsuitable, do what they musically prefer to do without us, ensuring our inessentiality and depriving themselves of what their education could and should provide to help them become what they desire to become musically.

In a democratic society people are enabled, through their general education, to decide for themselves what they want and need, on the basis of a comprehensive and balanced engagement with as many as possible of the diverse roles that their culture affords them, to enable them to discover which of them are most personally suitable. And they are enabled to develop their particular capacities and proclivities further, through specialized opportunities of as much diversity as can possibly be provided. The more diverse the opportunities to learn that we offer, the more the outcomes of cultural empowerment, service to cultural needs, and individual wholeness can be attained. I have suggested an education-wide ideal that is focused on precisely those outcomes and as a powerful antidote to No Child Left Behind: Each Child Fulfilled. Our unique and necessary contribution to that ideal is to enable each child, in his or her individuality, to be fulfilled musically.

Moving in the direction of representing music in the schools in all the many ways it is practiced and cherished outside of schools; that is, in all the many musical roles our culture provides, allows us to meet the musical needs of all, finally making us relevant to all. In general education in music, precisely where a program of comprehensiveness and balance in exploration of all the roles available to be played in our culture must take place, we have too often limited our offerings to a selection of proscribed approaches to musical learning that exist nowhere else in our culture except in the artificial world of many of our school music classrooms. In specialized electives, where the diversity of students' interests needs to be encouraged by an equal diversity of focused opportunities to learn, we have barely begun to break out of our traditional offerings, attractive to only a very small minority.

Staying the course—continuing to do what we are doing without adapting to new realities—is a dangerous strategy; a prescription for defeat. In our case we have the luxury of both staying the course, treasuring and protecting our established successes, while also setting forth into new and imaginative directions that can lead us toward wholeness, toward making, more effectively and realistically than we ever have, the genuinely comprehensive and balanced contribution that both music and students deserve to have made.

Our present program, in its success for the minority it serves, provides us with a powerful model for how to achieve comparable success in all the other musical opportunities that we have historically ignored. That is another reason, in addition to serving so well the interests of those who do take advantage of it, to cherish what we have done and to ensure its continuance and health. It is not what we *have* done that is threatening us. It is what we have *not* done that has progressively rendered us irrelevant to the musical realities of the majority of youngsters and adults.

Leadership for both preservation *and* innovation is needed to help us achieve the wholeness that has escaped us. That leadership will require us to dramatically revise our long-standing assumptions about the kinds of people we need to recruit into the music education profession, people whose passion to teach music is as variegated as is music itself. We will need to educate these musically diverse people in ways that both develop their expertise in the particular role or roles that they will represent, and to ensure that their understandings of music allow them to teach for breadth as well as depth, for seeing their special perspective in music as being one part of a larger whole. We will have to broaden the perspectives of teachers in service, to help them place their teaching in the larger contexts of music while retaining their special strengths in their specialization. We will have to conduct research on a far greater diversity of musical roles than we do at present. We will need to reform our advocacy efforts toward clarifying and celebrating the enhanced opportunities to learn that we are striving to make available. All this along with a variety of other initiatives that will break new and fertile ground upon which we can nurture our more complete, more vital professional purpose.

Are we up to that leadership, individually and as a profession with the help of our national association? I deeply hope that 100 years from now our 2007 centennial year will be regarded as the dawn of a new era for music education. In this new era our resolve to face the musical realities we have disregarded for too long, our imagination to conceive ways to represent fully the diversities of our rich, colorful musical culture, and our actions toward creating programs serving the needs, finally, of all students, will lead us to a more mature, more fulfilling, more universal and therefore more basic profession of music education than we have ever before achieved. I wish us, at the time of our hundredth birthday, the courage to advance our vision.

4

Are We There Yet? Why Not?

Paul Lehman

In 1984, when I was president of MENC, the National Executive Board adopted three goals for 1990. The first goal was the key. It said this: "By 1990, every student, K–12, shall have access to music instruction in school. The curriculum of every elementary and secondary school, public or private, shall include a balanced, comprehensive, and sequential program of music instruction taught by qualified teachers."

We fell short of that goal in 1990, and we're not there yet. But it's still a worthy goal, and it still reflects what I think we all want for the young people of America.

Let's get right to the fundamentals. You and I know that music and the other arts should be a part of the basic education of every student. Lots of people agree with us. So why hasn't it happened? What conditions have to be met before we can reach our goal? Well, here's my list. I've identified six conditions.

CONDITION 1: A CURRICULUM THAT IS TRULY BALANCED AND COMPREHENSIVE

First of all, we need a music curriculum that is truly balanced and comprehensive. Our challenge is not just to find a better way to market our product. It's also to build a better product. Bennett Reimer spoke about this very effectively. We need a curriculum that truly reflects the breadth of the national standards. This is the most important condition of all. It has to be the first priority. And our programs have to be designed for all students, not just the talented.

Some people still think of music in school as a frill. That idea has always been the crabgrass on the lawn of the music program. It persists because when it comes to the arts the line between education and entertainment is often fuzzy. Music plays a fundamental and pervasive role in show business and in popular culture, and that role often blinds people to the very different role it plays in education.

But our standards give us a powerful weapon to counter that misperception because they offer a coherent vision of what it means to be educated in music, and they place the emphasis not on methodology or repertoire or entertainment but squarely on student learning, where it belongs.

Music can't be a frill because ultimately schools exist to transmit our cultural heritage to the next generation, and music is one of the most powerful, and most treasured, and most glorious manifestations of every cultural heritage. Any student who is allowed to leave school without the formal study of music has been cheated just as surely as if he or she had been allowed to leave without studying science or math.

CONDITION 2: A RATIONALE FOR MUSIC IN SCHOOLS THAT IS SHORT, SIMPLE, AND CONVINCING

We need a rationale for music in schools that's short, simple, and convincing. We need a rationale that will persuade Joe Sixpack.

Our *Opportunity-to-Learn Standards* call for at least ninety minutes of music per week in the elementary school, and they call for music to be required through grade 8. If we want to be taken seriously, we have to answer the question "Why?"

We've had many rationales in the past. One of the best is provided in the MENC publication *Vision 2020*. But it's twenty-six pages long—and it has twenty-one footnotes. And I'll bet Joe hasn't read it. It's a great statement, and we need statements like that. There's an audience for that statement. But Joe is part of a different audience. And we need a rationale directed to him.

We've all drawn up lists of reasons why music should be taught in schools. We can probably cite twenty-seven reasons, but one or two reasons ought to be enough if they're good ones. The rationale I envision is no more than a paragraph long. I don't know exactly what it will say, but I think we're on the right track when we emphasize that music enhances the quality of life.

It's harder to write a short statement than a long one, but we can't allow our rationale to become merely a collection of all the pet slogans of every group in our coalitions because then it would be too lengthy and too unfocused to be effective.

It's especially hard to make this statement short because there are many stakeholders in education, and each one has a different view of the purpose of education. So a rationale that satisfies one group may not satisfy the others. For example, some people seem to think that the primary purpose of education is to prepare kids for jobs. I don't believe that at all. Employability is an important by-product of education, but not its major goal.

The nature of work has become so specialized and it's changing so rapidly that employers want to train their own employees. What they want from the schools are graduates who are trainable, and that means graduates with a solid background in the basic disciplines, including the arts. If we give kids that background, they'll get jobs. It's ironic that the skills employers value most highly all happen to be important outcomes of arts instruction—namely, creativity, discipline, flexibility, and skill in working cooperatively with others. There's nothing taught in the schools that develops those skills better than music.

In my view, the primary purpose of education is not preparation for jobs; it's the pursuit of truth and beauty, and the development of human capacities, and the improvement of the quality of life. And nothing does more than music to further these goals. Schools ought to focus on preparing kids for rich, satisfying, and rewarding lives, not for narrow roles in manufacturing and marketing consumer goods. And the way to do that is to focus on the basic disciplines, which include (1) math, (2) language and literature, (3) the physical sciences, (4) social studies, and (5) the arts.

Our young people aren't merely pawns on the gigantic chessboard of international economic competition. Earning a better living is less important than living a better life. Success doesn't just mean earning money; success means being able to live your life as you want to live it. Remember that education is what we have left over when we've forgotten the things we learned in school.

I'm looking forward to Don Hodges's comments during the Centennial Congress on the "Sounds of Learning" Project. I think this work is tremendously exciting, and I hope the results will show far-reaching benefits for music instruction. But whatever they show or don't show will have no effect on the ability of music to enhance the quality of life. Music will remain inherently valuable and worthwhile for its own sake.

CONDITION 3: IN THE HIGH SCHOOL, A DIVERSITY OF COURSE OFFERINGS THAT ATTRACT LARGE NUMBERS OF STUDENTS

At the high school level we desperately need a diversity of course offerings that attract large numbers of students. We've done a magnificent job of building instrumental and choral groups, and we can be very proud of that, and we ought not retreat one step from those accomplishments. But now it's time to expand on that foundation. This is simply part of our effort to build a curriculum that's truly balanced and comprehensive.

One reason this is important is that there are students in every school who are genuinely interested in music and want to study it but can't because they lack the background or interest or ability to be in band or orchestra or chorus, and there are no other courses available. Maybe they want to play guitar or keyboard. Some of them know a lot about popular music or ethnic music. Some have their own performing groups.

Even more important, the students we're not reaching include many of our brightest young people. In just a few years they'll be our principals and school board members and state legislators. These are the people who'll be making the decisions that affect our programs. It's suicidal to freeze them out.

Another of MENC's goals for 1990 was that every high school shall require one credit in the arts for graduation. Today that's a requirement in thirty-seven states—although sixteen of those states provide convenient loopholes. Oklahoma requires two credits—but with a wealth of alternatives. The District of Columbia requires a half credit in music.

The students in those thirty-seven states represent a huge market for new courses in music. We can ignore them and their schools will find some way for them to meet the requirement—perhaps with woodworking or synchronized swimming or something. But if we don't take advantage of these requirements to reach out to this broader student population we'll have missed an opportunity that comes literally once in a lifetime. We may have to begin modestly because of limited staff time, but once we demonstrate demand, resources will follow.

CONDITION 4: A PUBLIC FAMILIAR WITH THE CONTENT OF THE MUSIC PROGRAM

We need a public familiar with the content of the music program. What does the average citizen really know about what goes on in our classrooms? Not much, I'm afraid. Many think the entire program consists of what they see on the football field on Friday nights, or on the concert stage two or three times a year. We've had some success in filling this knowledge gap through "Music in Our Schools Month" activities. After an orientation for choir parents one mother was overheard saying to another "I didn't know they actually learned things in choir; I thought they just sang."

Still, there are far too many parents who did not themselves experience firsthand the joy and satisfaction of a high-quality music program in school. So they don't realize what their kids are missing. That's also true of too many principals. And the cycle is self-perpetuating. We have to break this cycle of musical malnutrition. We cannot afford another generation starved of the joy and beauty of music.

I think most people are willing to be convinced—even Joe Sixpack. And, happily, we have a vast array of allies willing to help, including every major participant in the education reform movement at the national level. But that support doesn't automatically filter down to the local level. For example, the National Association of Elementary School Principals supports the arts 100 percent, but that doesn't mean that the principal in your local elementary school does. We need to find ways to translate support at the national level into support at the grassroots level.

Polls show that the public too supports arts education. Parents want their kids to know the contributions of Mozart and Michelangelo as well as those of Newton and Einstein. Our support is a mile wide, though sometimes only an inch deep.

One of the best channels of communication open to us is standards-based grading. A grade is not just misleading, it's outright fraudulent if it means merely that the student has come to class, or tried hard—or, more accurately, given the appearance of trying hard. The most meaningful way to report student achievement to parents is to provide a profile indicating the student's progress toward each of the district's goals or standards. Standards-based grading requires a more complex reporting format than many schools now have, and it's something we can't do all by ourselves, but it's something we need to work toward.

CONDITION 5:
A MORE SUPPORTIVE PROFESSIONAL ENVIRONMENT

If we're to build a curriculum that's truly balanced and comprehensive and offer courses that appeal to large numbers of students, we need a more supportive professional environment. First of all, there have to be changes in our teacher education programs. We tend to teach as we were taught, and we teach what we were taught. We can't be expected to teach skills and knowledge we've never learned.

We also need vastly expanded opportunities for in-service professional development. Colleges and universities, professional groups, and school districts all have a role to play. There's an enormous gap between the recognized need and the reality. Would you want to be treated by a doctor who's had as few in-depth opportunities to update his skills since he left school as most teachers now have?

Perhaps the most common excuse we face in making music universal is that there's not enough time. I'm tired of hearing that. It's a phony claim. John Goodlad told us how to find the time in his book *A Place Called School*. So did the National Education Commission on Time and Learning in its report called *Prisoners of Time*.

But never mind that. There are schools all around us, in every state, that have no trouble finding time for music. And if school A can do it, school B can also. The fact is that all schools have the same amount of time. Some schools have more money. Some have better facilities. Some have newer equipment. But time is the one resource—the only resource—that is allocated with absolute equality to every school in the nation. Some don't use it all and some don't use it well, but it's there if they want it. The problem is not a lack of time; it's a lack of will masquerading as a lack of time.

Another flimsy excuse is that "the schedule won't allow it." Well, who's running this school anyway? Is it the schedule? Which makes more sense: To begin with a schedule and try to fit in learning experiences when and where we can? Or to begin with what we want kids to know and be able to do and then work out a schedule to make that possible?

Lack of funding is another classic excuse. First we have to gain acceptance of the idea that the arts belong among the basic core disciplines, and we've had some success in this. Congress has defined the basics to include the arts. But the job isn't finished until Joe Sixpack thinks of them that way as well.

We say we want the world's best schools; we just don't want to pay for them. Funding is a problem in every school program, but since the arts are among the basics they have to be funded in the same way that we fund the other basics. It is not acceptable to support certain basic programs with tax funds and make others rely on candy sales and car washes. That would be unthinkable in a society that truly valued education.

Some people complain that education is expensive. But compared to ignorance, it's a bargain. It's time for a surge strategy with respect to school funding.

CONDITION 6: A PLACE FOR MUSIC EDUCATORS AT THE TABLE WHEN EDUCATIONAL ISSUES ARE DISCUSSED

Most music teachers would rather just teach kids than mess around with advocacy and government relations. But education is essentially a political process so we can't just go in the music room and hide. We need to have a place at the table when education issues are discussed, and that requires an effective presence in the political arena.

There's mounting evidence, for example, that the testing requirements of NCLB, the No Child Left Behind Act, are causing some schools to cut back on time devoted to music and art in order to spend more time on reading and math. The law requires testing to determine whether kids are making so-called adequate yearly progress. But with a stunning lapse of common sense it leaves it up to the states to define what that means.

And it gets worse: the law further requires that all students be proficient in reading and math by 2014. No one who ever taught in a classroom could conceive of something so monumentally naive. The only way to do that is to set the proficient level so low as to be laughable. NCLB not only allows the states to manipulate the test results and mislead the public, it virtually requires them to do so. And meanwhile all of this demands so much testing that it distorts the curriculum and squeezes out the humanities. Trying to improve education simply by requiring tests is like trying to eliminate crime by making it illegal.

Education in our country is a state and local responsibility but it's a national concern. Our decentralized system allows sloppy practices and low achievement levels to pass unchallenged. That's one reason we need the leadership and coordination that groups like MENC can provide. Concerning standards, for example, ask yourself this: What does a kid in Florida or California need to know that a kid in New York or Illinois doesn't need to know? You can ask that question for any discipline or any state, and there's simply no good answer.

Our state organizations can exert leadership and influence as well. Kentucky has a high-stakes state assessment, and music items have been included for the past fifteen years. Every school receives a numerical grade as a measure of accountability based on how well its students do on the assessment. And get this: the results in music account for 4.75 percent of every school's grade at the elementary level and 7.13 percent of the grade at the secondary level. That's a powerful incentive for schools to strengthen their music programs, and it happened largely through the efforts of the Kentucky Music Educators Association.

Let me suggest that maybe the time has come for us to be more assertive in demanding that states and districts meet their obligations with respect to arts education. Many state constitutions require that the state provide "a comprehensive basic education" or words to that effect, and courts have held that "a comprehensive basic education" includes the arts. In some schools specific existing requirements are clearly not being met. Why do we tolerate this? In the past twenty years we've seen a number of lawsuits alleging that school districts were failing to satisfy various requirements, and many of these suits have been successful.

Is there a major discrepancy in your district between what's required and what's actually happening? Arkansas requires forty minutes of music a week. Texas requires "sufficient time for teachers to teach and students to learn the curriculum." That sounds like an opening in need of exploring.

Suppose that a group of parents were to bring legal action to force compliance with some existing requirement. There are certainly law firms that would be glad to help with this on a pro bono basis. Some of these lawyers are parents of our students. Teachers can't do this, but parents can. A few well-chosen, highly publicized cases could have a dramatic effect. Even if the result were dropping the requirement that would end the glaring hypocrisy of pretending that our kids are being taught music when in fact they're not.

Ultimately the most important battles in the struggle for music education will be fought not in Washington and not in the state capitals but district by district throughout the nation's 14,229 school districts. Remember, it was through local pressure that music first made its way into America's schools in 1838, and it will be through local pressure that music will remain there.

The bottom line is this: Music makes a difference in people's lives. We music educators have something to give to the youth of America that no one else can give them, and it's something that, once given, can never be taken away. It's the joy and beauty and satisfaction of music.

Music enhances the quality of life. Music exalts the human spirit. Music is vitamin M. Music is a chocolate chip in the cookie of life.

All we're asking is that the kind of music programs available in the best schools be made available in every school. How could a democratic society settle for anything less?

I'm still thinking about MENC's first goal for 1990. We're not there yet, but I'd like to think that maybe today we understand better why not, and maybe we're more able and willing to satisfy the prerequisite conditions. We won't reach utopia, but if we work as hard in the future as our predecessors did in the past, maybe, someday, we can reach some sort of Magic Kingdom of our own, beyond the one that lies just down the road from here.

5

Thinking and Acting on Behalf of Music Study

Samuel Hope

It is a mark of realism and courage for MENC to pose the question it has posed as a theme of this centennial conference. Why, after all we have done that is obviously good, after all the evidence that we have collected and presented, after all the rhetorical and even operational support that we cherish and reflect, why after all of this do we have so much trouble justifying music study in the schools?

These are not the questions of a self-satisfied profession. Indeed, these are questions of disappointment bordering on frustration. I have been asked to reflect on this theme question from a policy perspective. Given the pressures of time, I will concentrate on fundamentals rather than details. I have chosen four fundamental areas that I wish to speak about briefly. They are: recognition, protection, creativity, and strategy.

RECOGNITION

Let us begin with recognition and look at it from several perspectives. First, a thing has to be recognized before it can be valued. In our society, and worldwide, music is recognized and valued. The same is true to a lesser extent for music study. All of us here recognize that there is a distinction between valuing music and valuing music study. But, as our question of the week reveals, we do not know enough about how to make this distinction understood. Our problem is fundamentally one of ideas, the ideas people have about music study. Our policy orientation therefore needs to be fixed on changing minds, not just changing slogans or promotional techniques. The problem is complex because there is more than one mind.

Second, recognition involves understanding, respecting, and being grateful for the work that people do and the achievements produced by that work. Here are three fundamentals: (a) there are things that we can achieve better together than by ourselves, (b) our work as individuals is supported by our work in common, and (c) almost nothing we have now created itself.

The state of music education today is the result of efforts by thousands of people over long working lifetimes. Think about this for a moment. None of us here has any way to know the magnitude of the support that our efforts have received from just the people sitting in this room, much less all the other professional musicians and music teachers who have worked in the United States over the last 100 years. It is impossible to know all of the things MENC has done over that time that supports the work each of us does today. The same is true of our other national associations devoted to music study, such as Music Teachers National Association (MTNA), College Music Society (CMS), National Guild of Community Schools, the Network of Arts Education Schools, and the National Association of Schools of Music (NASM). Different organizations take obvious leadership in certain areas of concern. Without the leadership of MENC, most probably we would not have the voluntary National Standards for Arts Education of 1994. And even if we did have a set of standards, they would not be nearly as substantive and therefore effective as the ones we have today.

Third, in addition to recognizing the value of music study, and the work of others, we must also recognize realities that affect us. We live in times and contexts that produce illusions about accomplishment. Our technologies, our fatigue with organizational mechanics, and our frustrations about time can lead us to the conclusion that we can do it all by ourselves or with a small group of like-minded friends. In a nation organized as a democracy, where national and federal initiatives can matter a great deal, this position is not wise. When crises arise, there is usually not time to gather and organize all the forces needed. It is essential to be organized in advance, individually, locally, statewide, and nationally. Strength at every level is important.

There is one last perspective on recognition, and that is recognition of greatness. I begin with an advertisement from The Teaching Company for a set of lectures on calculus: "One of the greatest achievements of the human mind is calculus. It deserves a place in the pantheon of our accomplishments with Shakespeare's plays, Beethoven's symphonies, and Einstein's theory of relativity." It seems that individuals at The Teaching Company recognize truly great achievements in music as having intellectual parity with great mathematical and scientific achievements. How proud or willing are we to make the same statement as The Teaching Company to parents, students, and the public? To what extent is it clear to the public that we recognize and value the greatest achievements in our field, wherever they come from? We cannot make the headway that we should if we do not constantly connect music study, great achievement in music, and common effort on behalf of both. It is precisely these connections that are publicly understood for every discipline truly considered basic.

PROTECTION

I have already alluded to the importance of working together. When we work together, we Americans like to think about advancement more than protection, but protection is a critical ingredient in advancement. We protect our health in part so that we can continue to work and play and otherwise enjoy productive lives. We protect our field to some extent by advancing it. Nothing does succeed like success. But as our problem of the week reminds us, we are not able to advance unimpeded. There are many barriers to a full realization of our potential. There are concepts and specific proposals that are not in our interests. We need to protect music study from these things. Most often, we cannot do this by ourselves. The outside forces are too strong.

In developing policies that guide our efforts to protect, we have to think long and hard about when and how to say yes, when and how to say no, and even when and how to say maybe, or partially yes and partially no.

Over the years, there have been many ideas, forces, and policies associated with the arts and arts education that are good in and of themselves but that do not increase public recognition and therefore, public valuing of music study. In other words, every proposal that has "the arts," or "music" in it, is not necessarily good in terms of encouraging individual study and learning. Some of these proposals we have said "no" to outright. Some others, we ought to have challenged more. But this is not always easy because there are some things that seem good for music and for education that we want to say yes to because we want music or general education to succeed. But by saying yes without sufficient qualification or amendment, we often allow real music study to be subordinated to other arts- or education-related purposes. The result: public misunderstanding of music study grows.

We lose ground when we do not define our terms or our goals clearly enough to be able to debate and say no when things that sound good actually harm our ability to maintain public recognition and therefore valuing of music study. A clear example: there is nothing wrong with using music to teach other subjects. But if teaching other subjects is considered by the public as the primary function of music in the schools, we are obscuring recognition and valuing of music study itself. No field can promote its cause effectively if it regularly agrees or appears to agree that it has no principal function, if it is only secondary, supportive of other things.

In policy, there are other areas where the field needs protection. Governmental action is an obvious one. However, governmental action is also based on ideas that come from values and what is valued. And so, we need to remember that if a field is fragmented with regard to its core purposes, if a field does not prioritize its own strategic necessities effectively so that it is guided by reality in decision making, if a field does not protect itself in terms of fundamental ideas of what is at its center, that field is vulnerable to constant political and social action against its interests. National organizations like MENC exist, in part, to maintain essential protections, first in the world of ideas, and then in terms of operational mechanisms and capacities.

CREATIVITY

Let us now turn to creativity. There are many lessons about creativity that we can learn by just observing our own field. For example, much of our music is either written down completely or partially, or passed on through tradition. That which is written down or passed on is held in common. But then what happens? Each musician takes what is given and creates with it and from it. Interpretations and improvisations are different. In other words, we have a great deal of practice in creating frameworks and then creating within them, and in using our experience of doing one to inform our ability to do the other. Thus, we understand standards as a framework that need not lead to standardization. This realization seems impossible for many creating policies that affect education.

As a result, unfortunately, music education, like all other preK–12 education, lives and works in an environment where there are many anti-creative forces. Our field is the victim of ever increasing bureaucracy and regulatory control that little by little replaces the framework concept with rigid and extensive sets of rules for all teachers to follow. Creative people do not like to live and work in such circumstances; and so, many never engage, and many others leave.

There are many internal values and external practices that also hamper creativity in our society as a whole. Here are a few: the continuing success of many traditional or slowly evolving ways of doing things, inflexible government regulations, the infrastructures and interests associated with certain concepts or ways of working, common agendas and methodologies of funders, benchmarking, criteria used in rating systems and testing, exchanges of methodology facilitated by the internet, continuous promulgation of a "best practices" ethos, political correctness, and competition. The last statement made may not seem correct, that competition is a generator of sameness, but some years ago a wise friend observed, "Have you ever noticed that all the cars in the same price range essentially look the same?"

I sense that the problem posed for your consideration this week reflects a growing impatience with the way things are. Such impatience for change can be good if it is channeled productively and does not result in music education professionals turning on each other, refusing to recognize the achievements of the past, or failing to maintain the common efforts necessary for protection and security. We must create our way forward, being very careful not to break or damage something that we need.

Regarding creativity, I have been asked by the organizers of this conference to speak for a moment about the recent action of the NASM membership to approve changes to the standards for music teacher preparation. To be as brief as possible, NASM has now made more explicit its traditional position that there are many effective ways to prepare teachers, that there are many valuable bodies of content, and that many methods work well. Different situations and different teachers need to use different approaches to music study. Traditionally, the field has been divided into general, choral, and instrumental specializations. The new NASM standard adds a fourth category which provides tremendous flexibility to establish music education programs centered around other music specializations or performance genres or combinations thereof. NASM standards now explicitly support creative approaches to music teacher preparation. The expanded framework provides more room than ever for individual and institutional creativity. All of us understand that such an approach is not reflected in most state requirements and that liberalization there is a next challenge. NASM is grateful to MENC, the Society for Music Teacher Education (SMTE), and others in the music education professions who advised and supported NASM as it developed, reviewed, and ratified this important standards change.

STRATEGY

Let us turn now to strategy. So far in this talk we have considered the relationship between recognition and valuing, the importance of working together to protect ourselves and advance our cause, and the fundamental need to protect and develop conditions conducive to individual and organizational creativity. And all along, we have been indicating that MENC and other national organizations are an essential part of achievement in all these areas, and that they are essential meeting grounds accomplishing goals and objectives in all of these areas. The same is true for strategy. Strategy, policy, and their relationships are vast topics, so let us think together about six strategic necessities.

First, we must pursue the kind of wise policy making that involves both understanding and action. Action without understanding often results in wrong or ineffective moves that make the problem worse. Understanding without action leaves the problem unattended to grow as it will.

Second, as we seek to understand and act, we must review our ideas against a set of transcendent values. As a field, we must know what we cannot afford to lose. Otherwise, it is perfectly possible to make short-term gains at the expense of long-term losses. Fads, trends, and projects will always beckon. The cause of music study is perpetually in negotiations and engaged daily on a public relations battlefield. We must know what we must protect at all costs as we make decisions about promoting music study in a constantly changing situation.

Third, we must become more capable at defining the problems we face, particularly in terms of the ideas that generate and sustain them. For example, what ideas are reducing recognition and valuing for music study? Where are these ideas coming from? How can we counter or bypass these ideas or their sources? These are the kinds of questions that can lead to the understanding needed as the basis for effective action.

Fourth, we must recognize the importance of using a range of techniques for advancing public understanding of music study and its value. We need to counter many ideas from many sources; therefore, there is no silver bullet. One argument does not fit all. There is no single methodology. Many different messages, approaches, and levels of sophistication are needed, all working in parallel. We must make the most thoughtful judgments about what we say to whom. We must consider what we are teaching about our own values by what we say and do. In other words, we need to choose the best approach for specific places and times. Standard public relations techniques are important but not everything; intellectual debate, policy analyses, and proposals for quiet, long-term efforts are also essential.

Fifth, we must lift up the power of music itself and channel it to support public understanding of music study. Performances alone will not convince, but if excellent performances are linked to the learning that produces them, public understanding of music study and its value can be strengthened. We need to think more about how to enhance this important possibility and then act accordingly.

Sixth, we must take greater advantage of an important feature of our present condition, the potential influence of the local music teacher. Our teaching colleagues are already the most numerous and powerful advocates for music study. In the aggregate, they have regular access to millions of people. What can be done to help individual teachers raise their proficiency at developing public understanding beyond what they do naturally by teaching music? Effectiveness means being able to choose and mix messages and approaches for specific times and places, and even for specific individuals. Therefore, our national strategic goal in this area is not a common technical system, but rather a support mechanism that helps individuals and small groups at the local level become as adept at choosing and mixing messages and approaches as they are at teaching music itself.

CONCLUSION: RECOGNITION, PROTECTION, CREATIVITY, STRATEGY

None of us will be present for the 200th anniversary of MENC. We do not know exactly what will happen tomorrow much less a hundred years from now. But we do know our task, and we must pursue it with patience and faith. Literally, we must compose our way forward using transcendent values about music study as the basis for understanding and action as time and conditions evolve. If we are successful, a hundred years from now, our successors will be working on another problem. For their sakes and for the future of music study and its meaning for our young people, I hope this is the case. And so, let us go forward individually, locally, statewide, and nationally so that we develop a strong basis for this valuable and important achievement and do so in the great cause of advancing civilization in all its variety, richness, and power.

6

Changing the National Environment for Music Education from the Perspective of School Boards

Anne L. Bryant

I bet there's not a person in this room who believes that music education is not a fundamental part of every child's K–12 experience. And I'll bet that the schools you went to, I went to, and the schools that our children either are at or have been to had rich music and art education. I remember my blue-haired teacher—that was a long way back, and it was blue for the reasons it was blue in the 1950s. Looking back again, she was not a great teacher, but I loved the class. I also remember five years of piano lessons. I will tell you that they didn't work, although I can read music, pick out a tune, and I'm really glad I had it because I admire talented pianists. And I will also tell you that my daughter would not have graduated from high school had it not been for wonderful singing and acting programs at her public school.

I am not here to talk about the value of music education. You know the value, and Governor Huckabee was eloquent about it. We're here because of our commitment to music education and the arts. We want to talk about some of the harsh realities that we know you face and we face at the state and local levels. We want to address public attitudes like those people who fail to see their value and who don't support local efforts. The fact is that 75 percent of adults don't have kids in the public schools. They're the ones voting on bond issues, and they're the ones voting on, in many states, the school district budgets. When I talk to school board members about the barriers to rich music education in schools, the bottom line is always, "Anne, it's resources, it's money."

That leads me to the actual question, which is, "What are our priorities?" No one has all the money in the world if they live in public education today. I have a slight disagreement with Governor Huckabee when he says, "All you have to do is get it in the law and mandate it and the funding will follow." For those of us who work at the national level, the federal level, we know that there are a lot of mandates, and the money doesn't follow. Nevertheless, it's not a bad idea. Forty-nine states, as you well know, have music standards. So I would argue that, given this era of No Child Left Behind, we've got to change the law. NSBA, the National School Boards Association, is working hard to change the No Child Left Behind law.

The NSBA is very much in sync with what needs to be changed in that law. NSBA introduced House 648, a bill that incorporates forty-two recommendations for change, which do not tinker around the edges as some of our national leaders say is all that's needed. Actually, there are fundamental changes we think are needed in the accountability system, in the nature of assessment, particularly around English language learners and special education. We think the sanctions got it wrong. We propose to change a lot of the sanctions. My argument would be that if we can get these changes in No Child Left Behind, there will be more focus and attention on the students who need help the most and on broadening the curriculum and enriching it. That's where music education comes in.

I also think that we need to look at some of the strategies we can use at the local level. I want to tell you about Andrea Peterson. How many of you have heard of her? Andrea Peterson is the National Teacher of the Year. She's a music teacher at the Monte Cristo Elementary School in Granite Falls, Washington. She says she got into teaching because she learned from the best—her dad, who taught special education and wood shop for almost forty years. She got married and created a family of teachers with her mother-in-law and her two sisters. Peterson is credited for using her creativity to help her teach music when money was tight.

In her ten years at Monte Cristo, she's integrated music education into other subjects. She took novels that students were reading and turned them into musicals. Musical notes became another way to explain fractions. Her teaching extended well beyond the school, and she created a music program that honored local veterans. Did you hear what the story said? Working with other teachers, reinforcing others' agendas, teaching math and reading, and reaching out to the community to invigorate it. But

I wonder. What were the hurdles she faced? What made it so tough for her? I will bet what gave her motivation and passion wasn't just her love of music. She saw a different end objective. She took her creativity and she turned it into a twenty-first-century skill approach.

Paul Houston mentioned a wonderful book that I also recommend to you, Daniel Pink's *A Whole New Mind*. Pink is a businessman. It is a great book because he talks about how important it is to a business to focus on creating and strengthening the right side of the brain—the creative part of the brain. Pink says we have to do this in children if we are going to be economically competitive in business and in global areas. We will never win any kind of global competition if we produce more accountants, more X-ray technicians, more engineers. These fields can't compete in terms of jobs or wages with India and China. We will lose that game. He argues that the reason we have become strong as a country and that we must become even stronger is the notion of creativity. Dan Pink loves to talk about designer toilet brushes, which I happen to think is a kick. But he says you go into a Target or into J. C. Penney and you will find designer toilet brushes for $12 to $15 and people buy them.

Our creativity, which, if Detroit gets smart, could actually design even better cars, has led this country's economy as well, just as in music and the arts. If you go online or into a record store in Tokyo you'll find American music, but it's also about business enterprise. I love the conversation I had with a Disney executive in this place about a year ago. I said to him, "Whom do you hire?" His answer? Not MBAs, not even math and engineer and technology people. He said, "I will hire a musician; I can teach them the other stuff. I will hire an artist; I can teach them the other stuff." That is an enlightened CEO. Believe it or not, there are many more like that person.

What are the hurdles? Why are we all making the same arguments over and over again about why music education is so important? I'd argue that it's about priorities. School boards are partly responsible, as are superintendents, as are parents. We have got to work with the community to pressure the local decision makers to have the right vision and goals, to have twenty-first-century skills very much on their minds. Twenty-first-century skills demand creative thinking, problem solving, innovation. And we've got to align the resources so that we have a lot more Andrea Petersons in our school systems. We've got to harness the community because the community is what in fact the school board will respond to. Eight years

ago, NSBA, with school board members at the local level, created something called the *Key Work of School Boards*. I'm going to briefly run
through this with you, because it's your weapon of mass instruction.

The *Key Work of School Boards* has a very simple premise. It is what
boards should be doing in their districts: setting the vision with community
input standards or goals, and here's where you come in. My argument is
that you've got to be at the table when the local district goals are set. The
goals are not just around reading and math. The goal should be that every
child, every year is exposed to music education and music instruction in
school. Every child, every year. Then, if that's a goal, how do you assess
it? And here's where a multiple choice test can't assess music education.
The creativity that you need to bring to the decision making table is about
how to assess this. If you've got some ideas, I'd love to hear more from
you. That drives an accountability system. Remember, the accountability
system is not just for kids, it's for the adults in the system too.

The superintendent is evaluated by the school board based on those
goals. Principals are evaluated by the superintendent based on these goals.
And school boards are evaluated on those goals at the voter box. If they
meet the goals, chances are they'll have a great platform for running for
reelection. Alignment is a very key part of this plan. Do the resources and
does the money match the goals? If the goal is as we stated, that every
child is exposed to music education every year, where are the resources?
If you don't have goals and assessments, there's no argument around
alignment, which is key.

The ideal climate for teaching and learning is that the kids love coming
to school; the teachers love coming to work. Music education and the arts
are a fundamental part of that collaboration. And here's where reaching
out to the community counts most. Ninety percent of the community cares
about music education in the schools and continuous improvement.

So that's a framework you can use in going back to school boards. Even
if they haven't heard of it, it makes so much sense. This is the work of
a governing board, and I urge you to become partners at the table with
superintendents, with teachers, and in your community to talk about what
the right goals are. It's the soundest strategy you've got. We know that
without music education and the arts we won't have the kind of adults that
will lead this world.

7

Changing the National Environment for Music Education from the Perspective of State Boards of Education

Brenda Lilienthal Welburn

You know when any organization or entity celebrates a milestone in their existence, to be included in that 100th celebration is really an honor. So I'm just delighted to be here and delighted to be in the presence of what is probably, inarguably the most talented group of educators in the nation.

When Anne Bryant and I worked together a few years ago, just listening to the national anthem made me go home and feel so patriotic because you sing and the music is there and it makes you stop and recall and remember that everything we do in our nation has music attached to it. When we have birthdays, when we get married, when we are buried, when we celebrate our birthday next month, the next week, everything we do we plan around music. Music is something that transcends race and gender and age and culture and nationality.

When I started to think about how we would talk to you today, I had to ask myself how is it that something that is so fundamental to everything that we do is not regularly and strongly articulated as a national value—and no matter what we say about how much we enjoy it and use it, it is not articulated as a national value. And, in fact, even remarks such as Governor Huckabee's are not heard in the presidential debates; we don't talk about these values a lot in the educational debate.

Fortunately, there is a sense that our curriculum has narrowed to the point that we are not doing all that we should do to provide a comprehensive education for every child and yet while we say that, we still are not necessarily putting the mechanisms into place to make that happen. You know, you walk down the streets and people have iPods and you sit on the planes and there's CDs. It is everything that we do and yet we don't seem to value it.

Some of you may be aware that in 2003 after a year-long study, my organization, the National Association of State Boards of Education, issued a report entitled *The Complete Curriculum: Ensuring a Place for the Arts and Foreign Language in American Education.* Now we are a fairly small organization and our target audience includes primarily state policy makers, so we don't use a lot of resources in marketing our products, we send them to our members, we try and track to determine the policy impact of what we've done.

But we've wrestled with ourselves as a staff on how to measure whether the things that we say and do in our publications really do matter. Someone suggested that we Google our own publications and so I Googled *The Complete Curriculum.* And there were over 25,000 places where people were citing *The Complete Curriculum.* People that we didn't know, people that we are not engaged with or interacting with on a regular basis and 25,000 may not sound like a lot on the Internet, but when you think about it as a document that was never marketed or really pushed, the fact that people are looking for solutions and looking for policy answers around these issues, you realize what a terrific opportunity it is to capitalize on the public's interest.

And at the same time, while we look at what happens nationally with our publications, we also talk to our members and they are concerned about a narrow curriculum that doesn't include music, that doesn't include the arts. And this is an opportunity to continue to look at those issues. And let me tell you where I think are your places of input and opportunity.

There are three things that are converging right now and I'll start with the state perspective, the federal government, and then the national environment overall. At the state level, a number of states are starting to review and look at the standards they passed many years ago. Standards-based reform and accountability did not begin with No Child Left Behind. Before the bill was ever passed, forty-nine states had standards. They are now at the place where they are starting to look at those standards again and so if your state is looking and considering revising its standards, you need to be a part of that discussion.

Recently, the Massachusetts Department of Education developed *Mass-Core*. It's a guideline for local districts, not a mandate, but *MassCore* is the next generation of standards and what it is students need to know and be able to do. It includes the sciences, math, and language arts, but guess what it doesn't include? It doesn't include music, it doesn't include art, it doesn't include physical education, it doesn't include second languages. We happen to be in the process of working with the Massachusetts State Board of Education in selecting the next superintendent, the next commissioner of education in Massachusetts. As a part of that, we have a place on our website for people to comment on what they think the skill set should be for the next commissioner.

The arts community has blown up that mailbox because they know in their state, they've just seen *MassCore* and *MassCore* doesn't include them. By any means necessary they're going to try and influence that. And I'm obligated to take that to the state board of education in Massachusetts to say, "I realize that this is not a conversation about *Mass-Core*, but you need to understand that there is a large voice in your state that's very dissatisfied with what's happening in your standards." And so you need to be very vigilant about seeing about what's happening with changes in your state standards and to continue to infuse yourselves in that conversation and in that debate.

The second area that I encourage you to be involved in is the reauthorization of the Elementary and Secondary Education Act. I deliberately call it the reauthorization of the Elementary and Secondary Education Act and not No Child Left Behind. No Child Left Behind is the name the current administration gave to the Elementary and Secondary Education Act. If we are to look at that major piece of legislation that first passed in the early 1960s as the federal voice about what should happen in elementary and secondary schools, then we need to talk about what happens with our curriculum, with the arts and with language as opposed to simply drawing attention to the unintended consequences that we've witnessed since the passage or the reauthorization five years ago.

Anne Bryant is absolutely right that we have spent an enormous amount of time talking about and looking at what are those things in the legislation that have adversely impacted instruction and teaching and learning and students' performance. We've not spent a lot of time saying this is the opportunity to once again put voice to what the federal role should be in education and to begin to look at the context of the whole child in this education environment and what they need.

The third area? Governor Huckabee alluded to high school reform, and we're starting to see that definition being expanded to secondary school reform. We know that high school is really kind of late to start to address the concerns that we have about children who drop out of school, so we're looking at it from a middle school perspective. But we're all aware that high school redesign and reform is being driven by the philanthropic community. A lot is happening at the state level as Governor Huckabee indicated, but those things happening at the state level are often being funded and generated by the philanthropic community. If forty states have grants from the Gates Foundation and most of our organizations, mine included, have grants from the Bill and the Melinda Gates Foundation, then the agenda that's driving high school reform is really being driven by a segment of the population that has not stepped out and endorsed and embraced music education, and so we hear a lot about the STEM—Science, Technology, Engineering and Mathematics—agenda.

The STEM agenda is driving so much of what's happening in high school redesign. It is the primary focus of Governor Napolitano in her presidency of the National Governor's Association. When you begin to raise the issue of other issues beyond STEM, we are told that we are in a global fight for our life, for our economic security and stability, and we have to make sure that this is what we focus on. I would push back and say that I'm a mother of an artist, of a child who is an actress. I'm the mother of a musician, a sound engineer who also creates music. If you had told me about the STEM agenda when I was helping to steer my children to their passion, it would not have resonated with me. So we can't expect it to resonate with parents who see that their children have other interests, other goals, and other talents. We don't want families and parents to say this agenda of the education system in this country doesn't include my child.

We talk about the dropout rate and we have to ask ourselves what is it that we do that doesn't inspire a student to want to exceed and excel. Narrowing the agenda to solely embracing the STEM agenda is a mistake. I'm not opposed to the STEM agenda. I understand its value and its importance; I just don't think it's enough. I've had the privilege of traveling to China, and at every stop I heard repeatedly, how do you teach creativity? And it's an oxymoron because creativity is stimulated and it's a gift—you don't teach it. And, since I was coming to Disney World, I decided that that I would challenge you to add something to the STEM agenda and that would be the MAGIC agenda—since this is the land of magic—and that's Music and Art Generate Inspiration and Creativity. That's the agenda that we need if the STEM agenda is to be successful and we want to continue that.

In closing, I want to say that I don't know how many of you saw the *Today* show last week. Mikhail Baryshnikov was on, and he's going to dance again. I remember sitting in the Kennedy Center watching him dance the *Nutcracker Suite* with my son when he was six years old and I said, "Do you like it, Damon?" He said, "If I say I like it, are you going to make me take dance lessons?" And I said, "No, son, I just want you to appreciate the beauty of it," and he said, "I really do, Mom." So I looked at Baryshnikov who now says he's going to dance again. Meredith Vieira asked him, "Why are you going to do that?" and he said, "Because I know what it is to embrace the arts." He said, "It's because you will change the world by expressing yourself honestly and artistically." And I do believe we can change the world by expressing ourselves honestly and artistically. You, as the music educators of our nation, are key to that.

Appendix A

Statement of Belief and Purpose, 1947

Original statement first published in the October 1930 Music Supervisors Journal. *Revised version, written by Osbourne McConathy (MENC president 1918–1919), adopted by the MENC biennial meeting in Los Angeles in 1940.*

Editorial Board: Edward B. Birge (*Chairman Emeritus*), Charles M. Dennis (*Chairman*), Lillian L. Baldwin, Glenn Gildersleeve, Mark H. Hindsley, Russel V. Morgan, Anne Grade O'Callaghan, Harold Spivacke, Paul Van Bodegraven
Editorial Associates: John W. Beattie, Peter W. Dykema, Will Earhart, Karl W. Gehrkens, Carl E. Seashore, Luis Sandi (Mexico), Domingo Santa Cruz (Chile)

Throughout the ages, man has found music to be essential in voicing his own innate sense of beauty. Music is not a thing apart from man; it is the spiritualized expression of his finest and best inner self.

There is no one wholly unresponsive to the elevating appeal of music. If only the right contacts and experiences are provided, every life can find

---

"Statement of Belief and Purpose," *Music Educators Journal* 34, no. 2 (1947): 17. The "Statement of Belief and Purpose" is from resolutions adopted by the Music Educators National Conference at its biennial meeting held in Los Angeles in 1940. The original statement, of which this is a simplified version, was first published in the *Music Educators Journal*, then the *Music Supervisors Journal* for October 1930.

in music some answer to its fundamental need for aesthetic and emotional outlet. Education fails of its cultural objectives unless it brings to every child the consciousness that his own spirit may find satisfying expression through the arts.

The responsibility of offering every child a rich and varied experience in music rests upon the music teacher. It becomes his duty to see that music contributes its significant part in leading mankind to a higher plane of existence.

The Music Educators National Conference, in full acceptance of its responsibilities as the representative and champion of progressive thought and practice in music education, pledges its united efforts in behalf of a broad and constructive program which shall include:

Provision in all the schools of our country, both urban and rural, for musical experience and training for every child, in accordance with his interests and capacities.

Continued effort to improve music teaching and to provide adequate equipment.

Carry-over of school music training into the musical, social, and home life of the community, as a vital part of its cultural, recreational, and leisure-time activities.

Increased opportunities for adult education in music.

Improvement of choir and congregational singing in the churches and Sunday schools; increased use of instrumental ensemble playing in connection with church activities.

Encouragement and support of all worthwhile musical enterprises as desirable factors in making our country a better place in which to live.

Appendix B

Yale Seminar on Music Education, 1963

Through a grant to Yale University, a seminar called "Music in Our Schools: A Search for Improvement" took place in 1963. A panel of 31 musicians, teachers, and scholars convened to discuss the kinds of music and repertoire that could improve music education.

MUSICIANS MEET AT YALE UNIVERSITY

A Seminar on Music Education was held at Yale University from June 17–28. The Seminar was supported through a contract with the United States Office of Education under the Cooperative Research Program.

The Seminar was unique from several standpoints:

1. For the first time a cross-section of music interests met together for an extended conference on music education. The thirty representatives at the conference included musicologists, composers, music educators, performing artists, performing jazz music artists, school administrators, music education administrators, ethnomusicologists, conductors, music critics.

"Seminar on Music Education: Musicians Meet at Yale University," *Music Educators Journal* 50, no. 1 (1963): 86–87.

2. Participants in the conference took full advantage of the opportunity to contribute their various abilities and from their respective fields of knowledge for the sole purpose of analyzing the role of music in education and education in music for all of the students in the schools.

Participants in the conference through extended discussions made every effort to channel their thinking and recommendations for the purpose of the advancement of the music instruction program in the schools with particular reference to contemporary life and culture.

The work of the Seminar was divided between plenary meetings to hear and discuss prepared papers, and sectional meetings concentrating upon six areas: (1) the teaching of music reading through making and writing music; (2) the widening of the musical repertory of performing groups in the light of recent historical and ethnological research; (3) the development of musical understanding through a study of music as a literature; (4) the utilization of composers and performers in residence; (5) the development of new educational media, such as films, tapes, and programmed instruction; (6) development of courses, resources, and activities for students who are more advanced musically than their contemporaries.

Following is a news release issued on the final day of the conference:

The conferees urged a greater use of creative activities in teaching reading and basic musicianship particularly in the elementary grades. This confirmed the success of teachers who had experimented with this medium of instruction as a result of two summer institutes at Bennington College supported by the American Council of Learned Societies in 1960 and 1962. A balanced program of activities, including music-reading, singing, playing, and listening under the direction of trained music teachers for all elementary school children was recommended as a long-range goal. Whatever repertory is used for these activities, it was emphasized, must be of the highest musical quality available. The conference deplored the wide-spread use of what was several times referred to as "pseudo-music."

For high schools a balanced program of courses and activities was recommended. These would include not only the present large performing organizations but also smaller ensembles that would permit greater individual initiative and would be more relevant to later amateur activity. Every large high school, it was urged, should offer opportunities for concentrated study of musical literature and theory, both on a level intended for the average student and for the pupil more advanced musically than his contemporaries. Courses in theory, it was suggested, should be exploratory and should lead through the pupil's own discovery of the materials of sound to a gradual understanding of its nature and possibilities. Courses in musical literature should avoid the survey by concentrating on few musical works which would be illumined by close analysis and by bringing to bear upon them other historically or functionally related music.

The range of the present repertory was found inadequate in terms of recent advances in musicology and composition particularly with respect to music before the eighteenth century, non-Western music, and contemporary music. One of the recurring themes of the conference was the need for music teachers and their pupils to regain contact with the musical world around them—the musics of the peoples of different parts of the globe.

The program of composers-in-residence begun under Ford Foundation sponsorship in 1959 and recently greatly expanded by a grant of $1,380,000 to the Music Educators National Conference was acclaimed as an important step in this direction. The conferees made a plea for a similar program of musicians and ensembles in residence to give school children contact with living examples of artistic refinement and excellence.

Various programs for implementing the Seminar's proposals were outlined, including the production of kits of materials for teachers and pupils, instructional and ethnological films, tapes containing programmed instruction, and other aids, research projects, and schemes for teacher training and re-training. These will be described in a report to the U.S. Office of Education being prepared by Claude Palisca, associate professor of the history of music at Yale and director of the Seminar.

"A most remarkable feature of the conference," Mr. Palisca stated, "was the degree of agreement reached by such a disparate group of people. They represented professions never brought together to consider the problems of music education . . . There emerged a strong sense of commitment to the release of the innate musicality and creativity of school children, the development of a deeper understanding of musical processes, and to a musical repertory of the highest quality in every area of performance and listening."

Composers represented were: Henry Brant, Bennington College; Lukas Foss, newly appointed conductor of the Buffalo Symphony; Leon Kirchner, Harvard University; Otto Luening, Columbia University; and Lionel Nowak, Bennington College.

Representing the concert field were: Adele Addison, soprano; Noah Greenberg, conductor; and Milton Katims, violist and conductor of the Seattle Symphony.

Radio, newspapers, and libraries were represented by Irving Lowens, specialist in American music, critic, and librarian, Library of Congress; Marcus Raskin, member of the Panel on Educational Research and Development of the executive branch of the Federal government; Eric Salzman, composer and music director of station WBAI-FM of New York; and Theodore Strongin, critic of the *Knickerbocker News* of Albany, New York.

Two jazz experts, Mercer Ellington of station WLIB, New York, and Billy Taylor of WNYC, New York, represented the field of jazz music.

Music education administrators were: Allen P. Britton, associate dean of the School of Music, University of Michigan; William B. McBride, head of music education, Ohio State University; Jerrold Ross, New York University; and Gid Waldrop, administrative officer, Juilliard School of Music.

Music as an academic discipline was represented by Edward T. Cone, composer and pianist, Princeton University; Mantle Hood, director of the Institute of Ethnomusicology of the University of California; Claude V. Palisca, musicologist, Yale University; Allen Sapp, composer, chairman of the Department of Music, University of Buffalo; and G. Wallace Woodworth, Harvard University.

Members of the music teaching and school administrator profession were: Herbert Alper, district music supervisor, Farmingdale, New York; Mrs. Earnestyne Mannatt, assistant superintendent of schools, division of elementary education, Los Angeles; Thomas Hilbish, Princeton High School; Evelyn Hunt, Dalton Schools; Ronald B. Thomas, Nanuet, New York, Public Schools; John Carton, Shirley Center, Massachusetts.

Musical theorists who participated: Howard L. Boatwright, Jr., who is also a violinist and composer, Yale University; and William J. Mitchell, Columbia University.

Observers were: Harold Arberg, specialist for music education, cultural affairs branch, U.S. Office of Education, Washington, D.C.; Edmund A.

Cykler, Department of Music, University of Oregon, Eugene; Herbert Haufrecht, music director, Young Audiences, Inc., New York; John Larenz, U.S. Office of Education, Washington, D.C.; Martin Mayer, Panel on Education Research and Development, New York; John Mays, National Science Foundation, Washington, D.C.; Bernard Fitzgerald and Vanett Lawler, MENC headquarters office, Washington, D.C.

Appendix C

Tanglewood Symposium, 1967

Sponsored by MENC, the Tanglewood Symposium, with its theme of "Music in American Society," picked up where the Yale Seminar left off. After discussion by musicians, sociologists, scientists, labor leaders, philosophers, representatives of government and foundations, music educators, and other musicians, the participants issued the Tanglewood Declaration calling for music to be placed at the core of the school curriculum.

THE SYMPOSIUM

An Introduction, by Robert A. Choate

Tanglewood, summer home of the Boston Symphony Orchestra, was the setting for an event unique in the annals of music in the United States. From July 23 to August 2, 1967, a fifty-member Symposium considered major concerns related to the theme, "Music in American Society." The Symposium was convened by the Music Educators National Conference in cooperation with the Berkshire Music Center, the Theodore Presser Foundation, and the School of Fine and Applied Arts of Boston University.

Robert A. Choate, Charles B. Fowler, Charles E. Brown, and Louis G. Wersen, "The Tanglewood Symposium: Music in American Society," *Music Educators Journal* 54, no. 3 (1967): 50–51.

Musicians, sociologists, scientists, labor leaders, educators, representatives of corporations, foundations, communications, and government and others concerned with the many facets of music assembled for this purpose. Discussions were based on critical issues, which had been identified by consultants and some 800 musicians, educators, and arts councils officials at the 1967 MENC Division Conferences.

In turn, the conclusions and recommendations of the Tanglewood Symposium were presented at the Interim Meeting in mid-August to officers of MENC State Associations, state supervisors, and other leaders in music education for their consideration and action. The final phase of the Symposium Project will constitute a major segment of the MENC biennial meeting in Seattle in March 1968.

Why was such a conference organized with participants of such diverse background and viewpoints? It is obvious that the entire music profession as well as other arts are now facing urgent problems. These challenges arise from social, economic, and cultural developments of the last several decades and emanate from an emerging ideology and maturing of the nation as a whole. The following broad issues were identified in position papers that appeared in the March and April 1967 issues of the Music Educators Journal. These served as bases for discussion in Division conferences and for the participants in the Tanglewood Symposium: What are the characteristics and desirable ideologies for an emerging postindustrial society? What are the values and unique functions of music and other arts for individuals and communities in such a society? How may these potentials be attained?

The Symposium sought to reappraise and evaluate basic assumptions about music in the "educative" forces and institutions of our communities—the home, school, peer cultures, professional organizations, church, community groups, and communications media—to develop greater concern and awareness of the problems and potentials of music activities in our entire culture and to explore means of greater cooperation in becoming more effective as we seek new professional dimensions.

During the first week of the Symposium, in plenary sessions, panel presentations, and through subject area discussions, the Symposium members explored "value" systems: the role of the arts in society; characteristics of the "emerging age": possible social, cultural, scientific, educational, and international developments; the music(s) of our time and trends in contemporary music; the impact and potentials of technology; economic and community support for the arts; potentials in the behavioral sciences; the nature and nurture of creativity; and means of cooperation among institutions and organizations concerned with music.

For three days, in a "post-session" limited to music educators and consultants, implications of the Symposium for music education were formulated. Critical issues were identified, and recommendations for action suggested. A "Tanglewood Declaration" was drawn. Implications and recommendations for the music curriculum, for educational processes, for evaluation, and for music in higher education and the community were made.

The following pages report in greater detail some of the concepts, ideas, suggested changes, and plans for further development that were formulated by the Symposium. An "interpretive" report is in preparation. A "documentary" report with full texts of presentations, group and committee reports and recommendations is being compiled. A filmslide and tape will be available soon. Together these sources convey some of the intense involvement, enthusiasm, and the stimulating "spirit of Tanglewood," and they afford a more complete and informative documentation of the materials that are presented on the following pages. These documents will be published by the MENC at the earliest possible time.

Gratitude is due MENC President Louis G. Wersen, the Board of Directors, and the cooperating institutions that made the Symposium possible. Acknowledgment is made of the significant contributions of the Symposium participants, consultants, and members of division discussion groups.

The full meaning and effectiveness of the Symposium Project remain to be seen; the study is open-ended and ongoing. The responsibility for implementation lies with MENC officers and members at local, state, and national levels. Dimensions and potentials for developments in music education have been identified. Recommendations have been formulated. Appropriate action now becomes a professional imperative.

The author is director of the Tanglewood Symposium Project and professor of music, School of Fine and Applied Arts, Boston University, Boston, Massachusetts.

THE TANGLEWOOD DECLARATION

The intensive evaluation of the role of music in American society and education provided by the Tanglewood Symposium of philosophers, educators, scientists, labor leaders, philanthropists, social scientists, theologians, industrialists, representatives of government and foundations, music educators and other musicians led to this declaration:

> We believe that education must have as major goals the art of living, the building of personal identity, and nurturing creativity. Since the study of music can contribute much to these ends, *we now call for music to be placed in the core of the school curriculum.*
>
> The arts afford a continuity with the aesthetic tradition in man's history. Music and other fine arts, largely non-verbal in nature, reach close to the social, psychological, and physiological roots of man in his search for identity and self-realization.
>
> Educators must accept the responsibility for developing opportunities which meet man's individual needs and the needs of a society plagued by the consequences of changing values, alienation, hostility between generations, racial and international tensions, and the challenges of a new leisure.

Music educators at Tanglewood agreed that:

1. Music serves best when its integrity as an art is maintained.
2. Music of all periods, styles, forms, and cultures belong in the curriculum. The musical repertory should be expanded to involve music of our time in its rich variety, including currently popular teen-age music and avant-garde music, American folk music, and the music of other cultures.
3. Schools and colleges should provide adequate time for music in programs ranging from preschool through adult or continuing education.
4. Instruction in the arts should be a general and important part of education in the senior high school.
5. Developments in educational technology, educational television, programmed instruction, and computer-assisted instruction should be applied to music study and research.

6. Greater emphasis should be placed on helping the individual student to fulfill his needs, goals, and potentials.

7. The music education profession must contribute its skills, proficiencies, and insights toward assisting in the solution of urgent social problems as in the "inner city" or other areas with culturally deprived individuals.

8. Programs of teacher education must be expanded and improved to provide music teachers who are specially equipped to teach high school courses in the history and literature of music, courses in the humanities and related arts, as well as teachers equipped to work with the very young, with adults, with the disadvantaged, and with the emotionally disturbed.

Appendix D

The Child's Bill of Rights in Music

MENC statement that every American child should have these rights to instruction in music.

MENC: The National Association for Music Education (formerly Music Educators National Conference) believes that every American child should have the following rights to instruction in music and urges that these rights be recognized and guaranteed by educational funding authorities, school administrators, and the public:

1. As their right, all children at every level must have access to a balanced, comprehensive, and sequential program of music instruction in school taught by teachers qualified in music.
2. As their right, all children must be given the opportunity to explore and develop their musical abilities to the fullest extent possible through instruction that is equal to that provided in the other basic subjects of the curriculum and is responsive to the individual needs of each child.
3. As their right, all children must receive the finest possible education in music, every child must have an equal opportunity to study music, and the quality and quantity of children's music instruction

Music Educators Journal 78, no. 8 (1992): center insert. Also found at www.menc.org/resources/view/child-s-bill-of-rights.

must not depend upon their demographical location, social status, racial or ethnic status, urban/suburban/rural residence, or parental or community wealth.

4. As their right, all children must receive extensive opportunities to sing, play at least one instrument, compose, improvise, and listen to music.

5. As their right, all children must have the opportunity to study music of diverse periods, styles, forms, and cultures, including samples of the various musics of the world and music that reflects the multidimensional nature of our pluralistic American culture.

6. As their right, all children must have the opportunity to develop their abilities to analyze music with discrimination, to understand the historical and cultural backgrounds of the music they encounter, to make relevant critical judgments about music and performances, and to deal with aesthetic issues relevant to music.

7. As their right, all children must have the opportunity to grow in music knowledge, skills, and appreciation so as to bring joy and satisfaction to their lives, challenge their minds, stimulate their imaginations, and exalt their spirits.

Original version adopted March 21, 1950
Revised version adopted November 1, 1991

Appendix E

The Power of the Arts to Transform Education:
An Agenda for Action

Recommendations from the Arts Education Partnership Working Group

Recommendations from the Arts Education Partnership Working Group about placing the arts on the nation's education agenda, from an effort chaired by James D. Wolfensohn, chairman of the John F. Kennedy Center for the Performing Arts, with Vice Chair Harold M. Williams, president of the J. Paul Getty Trust. Membership in the group included classroom organizations and national organizations in the arts and education, including John Mahlmann of MENC.

We present the recommendations of the Arts Education Partnership Working Group.

These actions will help place the arts on the nation's education agenda. Over the last decade, the belief has deepened that we must educate all our children to new levels of excellence. We speak for all the members of the Arts Education Partnership Working Group in affirming the conviction that the arts are essential to education, in our communities, and our schools.

We are convinced that excellence in education is possible only with the full inclusion of the arts. An education that encompasses and respects the wonderful diversity of peoples and cultures in the nation is possible only when it includes the arts.

The document from the Arts Education Partnership Working Group is available from www.eric.ed.gov/ERICDocs/data/ericdocs2sql/content_storage_01/0000019b/80/13/bb/a3.pdf.

69

The arts define what we mean by civilization. They are part of the foundation and framework of our culture. As a universal language through which we can express our common aspirations, the arts are a channel to understanding and appreciating other cultures. They are a basic and central medium of human communication and understanding. They encourage our children to dream and to create, to have beliefs, and to have a sense of identity within our rich and diverse culture.

The arts are unique ways of knowing and forms of knowledge. They are essential elements in the development of our children.

A society that deprives its students of these studies accepts mediocrity and endangers a democracy that depends on an informed citizenry to sustain it.

The full inclusion of the arts in education means the full use of all the cultural resources and arts organizations at local, state, and national levels. Theatres and dance companies, orchestras, museums and performing arts centers, local arts agencies and state arts councils all bring to education a wealth of knowledge and resources.

Working as partners, arts and cultural organizations and educators and schools complement and strengthen each other while bringing quite different skills and capacities to the larger goal of education reform. Such partnerships already exist in many locations, and they are an important source of reform and renewal for teachers, students, artists, schools, and communities.

By bringing together federal, national, state and local partners and sharing our talents, we bring to the education of our children the knowledge, the beauty and the vitality of the arts, enabling future generations of Americans to explore, to dream, to participate in our nation, and create its future.

We are optimistic about that future.

These recommendations are an open door; we need only the will and the determination to walk through it. We look forward to working closely with federal, national, state, and local partners to realize and implement them.

James D. Wolfensohn
Chairman
The Kennedy Center

Harold M. Williams
President
The J. Paul Getty Trust

RECOMMENDATIONS

To transform education, the working group makes the following specific recommendations for Congress and the administration. We urge collaboration among national, state, and local agencies and organizations to implement them.

I. A National Center for the Arts in Education

In considering the establishment of a national center, the working group acknowledges the many valuable programs across the nation. Still, it concludes that only a national center will enable the arts to contribute to education reform by providing a critical missing service to educators, artists and arts professionals, policymakers, and others by establishing and coordinating national resource exchanges and dissemination; that only a national center will develop and sustain a perspective inclusive of all the art forms and of a variety of approaches and strategies; that only a national center will serve as a means for the coordination of information and programs linking ongoing work in standards-setting, research, assessment, and other national developments; that only a national center will provide national visibility and signal a national commitment to the arts as fundamentally important to education.

The foundation for a national center is an information network that connects research, effective programs, and vital information with the people and communities who will use them.

A national center would support and enhance the work of local communities by enabling them to learn from each other and to base their own efforts on the best available information.

We recommend the establishment and funding to sustain a National Center for the Arts in Education.

The Center would perform the following functions:

- Serve as the coordination unit in a proactive national system for the gathering and dissemination of information resources on the arts in education;
- Facilitate coordination of national initiatives in support of the goal of making the arts a fundamental part of the general education of all students;

- Organize forums for discussion, analysis, and clarification of policies and issues important to understanding the contributions of the arts to excellence in education and the consideration of alternative approaches and actions;
- In cooperation with the national arts education research agenda, coordinate the national dissemination of research, facilitate its application, and identify and respond to gaps in these areas.
- Identify and recognize excellence and achievement by teachers, programs, schools, communities, and partnerships.

II. Professional Development and Teacher Education

Teacher education and preparation in the arts, both for new teachers and those who are already teaching, are critical to the achievement of the transformation of teaching and learning. We believe that teachers must work in partnership with colleagues and with the arts and education community outside the schools in order to transform successfully the role of the arts in education. This will require significant changes in the education, certification, and reeducation of teachers, including classroom teachers, specialists, and artists as educators. The key issues and recommendations in this report reside in the firm belief that reform of teacher education in the arts is critical to the success of national education reform.

We recommend support for the transformation of teacher education in the arts for both preservice and in-service.

We urge the creation and funding of a program for arts education comparable to the Eisenhower Program for Math & Science Education. The effort should:

- Initiate and fund pilot teacher-preparation programs that demonstrate what arts specialists and classroom teachers, individually and cooperatively, should know, be able to do, and value in the arts in order to reach K–12 students;
- Identify and support model programs that demonstrate how preservice arts education can be integrated with standards for teacher preparation;
- Encourage and support the development and strengthening of partnerships between the arts and education communities; and
- Encourage and support the involvement of artists, other arts professionals, and arts organizations in arts education.

III. Standards and Assessment

The transformation we envision creates new expectations for teaching and learning. Curriculum standards and student assessments make important contributions to meeting these expectations. Under the leadership of the National Committee for Standards in the Arts, standards for learning in the arts are now being established for the first time. Simultaneously, an effort to build consensus for a new assessment of the arts through the National Assessment of Education Progress (NAEP) is underway. The standards-setting process and the process of developing outcomes to be assessed are similar. Both need to identify what children should know and be able to do in the arts. Both need to be comprehensive in addressing a broad range of knowledge and skills in the arts. It is essential that there be close coordination as these two independent processes move forward.

The national voluntary curriculum standards need to be embraced and accepted by state departments of education and local education agencies as they develop or revise their curriculum frameworks and assessments in the arts to ensure that the standards have impact on the teaching and learning of the arts in the classroom, on teacher education, and/or on teacher certification. Whether the national standards and the arts assessment instruments are accepted as models to guide state and local education agencies will depend to a great extent upon an informed understanding of them.

We recommend that the Congress, the Department of Education, and other appropriate federal and state agencies:

- Support coordination between the arts curriculum standards-setting process and the arts assessment process;
- Support implementation of periodic national arts assessments;
- Support implementation by states and localities; and
- Seek inclusion of the arts in the National Educational Goals.

IV. Partnerships

We strongly believe that the power of the arts to transform education can succeed only with effective partnerships and collaborations. These must be built at local, state, and national levels. Successful education reform, especially efforts that incorporate the arts, depends upon informed community support. Partnerships bringing schools and educators together with arts and cultural organizations are an important element in building and sustaining community support. The most important partnerships are community based, for it is in the local community where support must be built to sustain reform. We believe that local partnerships, involving educators, arts organizations, parents, local decision makers, and all the members of a community, should be affirmed and supported.

We recommend that appropriate national programs be established to support and encourage all communities involved in education reform to:

- Include the arts in their goals;
- Involve arts educators and arts and cultural organizations in the planning and implementation; and
- Institute a program to identify, recognize, and disseminate information about community-school partnerships that use the arts for achieving excellence and for advancing education reform.

These programs may be implemented most effectively through the National Center for Arts Education.

We recommend that arts educators, including artists and arts organizations and agencies, commit themselves and their institutions to full and active participation in local, state, and national education reform efforts.

With our children in mind, in all their wonderful diversity and individual uniqueness, we urge the implementation of these recommendations.

In Conclusion

American children must be fully nurtured, affirmed, and enabled by the educational opportunities we provide. The arts are an indispensable resource for assuring these advantages and improving the opportunities that now exist. If our children are to prosper mentally and emotionally to their maximum, education reform must incorporate the arts and exploit their capacity to transform learning and teaching.

We conclude that the best strategy for making the arts essential to a basic education is for educators and artists, as well as schools and arts and cultural organizations, to work collaboratively towards comprehensive education reform.

For the benefits of the arts to be realized in current educational reform efforts, the leadership of the administration and Congress are imperative. The working group recognizes the arts as a potent ally in the challenging process of transforming American education and American schools. These recommendations could help the rich resources of the arts to be used to enormous educational advantage. Our children, our nation, and our future will be the beneficiaries.

BACKGROUND

In response to concerns from the education and arts communities about the absence of the arts from the National Educational Goals and to ensure their inclusion in subsequent education reform efforts, a number of actions and initiatives were taken to put the arts on the national education agenda. These included:

- Developing world-class standards in the arts;
- Implementing high national standards;
- Including communities involved in education reform;
- Including the arts in the National Assessment of Education Progress;
- Creating a National Center for Arts Education;
- Developing a research agenda in arts education; and
- Designing a National Arts Education Dissemination Network.

James D. Wolfensohn, chairman of the John F. Kennedy Center for the Performing Arts, convened a task force of private citizens to consider these initiatives and recommend actions. Wolfensohn asked Harold M. Williams, president of the J. Paul Getty Trust, to serve as vice chair and to support the effort. Together they formed the Arts Education Partnership Working Group.

Membership on the working group includes classroom teachers, principals, and superintendents; and representatives of theatres, dance companies, orchestras, museums, arts centers, state and local arts organizations, foundations, and other national organizations in the arts and in education.

The working group met for the first time on June 22, 1992, at the Kennedy Center. It considered the current initiatives outline and identified others important to bringing the full benefit of the arts into the nation's quest for educational excellence for all its children. In order to facilitate these efforts, the working group divided into the following six subcommittees:

- National Center Including Dissemination and Research
- Professional Development/Teacher Education
- Standards and Assessment
- Arts and Education Reform
- Advocacy and Partnership
- Other Strategies

The subcommittees worked over the summer of 1992 to prepare recommendations for the full working group, which met again in Los Angeles on October 18 and 19, hosted by the Getty Center for Education in the Arts.

As deliberations went on, the working group focused on the strong relationship between inclusion of the arts and overall education excellence. This is a summary of the work and the recommendations for action.

The Arts Education Partnership Working Group
Washington, D.C.
January 1993

Appendix F

National Standards for Music Education, 1994

On behalf of the Consortium of National Arts Education Associations, MENC received a grant from the U.S. Department of Education to develop voluntary national standards for each of the four arts disciplines—music, visual arts, theatre, and dance—in grades K–12. The National Standards were supported or endorsed by more than eighty national organizations.

SUMMARY STATEMENT:
EDUCATION REFORM, STANDARDS, AND THE ARTS

These National Standards for Arts Education are a statement of what every young American should know and be able to do in four arts disciplines—dance, music, theatre, and the visual arts. Their scope is grades K–12, and they speak to both content and achievement.

The Reform Context

The standards are one outcome of the education reform effort generated in the 1980s, which emerged in several states and attained nationwide

Consortium of National Arts Education Association, summary statement from *National Standards for Arts Education* (Reston, VA: MENC, 1994), 131–33. National Standards for Music Education (content standards), found at www.menc.org/resources/view/national-standards-for-music-education.

visibility with the publication of *A Nation at Risk* in 1983. This national wake-up call was powerfully effective. Six national education goals were announced in 1990. Now there is a broad effort to describe, specifically, the knowledge and skills students must have in all subjects to fulfill their personal potential, to become productive and competitive workers in a global economy, and to take their places as adult citizens. With the passage of the Goals 2000: Educate America Act, the national goals are written into law, naming the arts as a core, academic subject—as important to education as English, mathematics, history, civics and government, geography, science, and foreign language.

At the same time, the Act calls for education standards in these subject areas, both to encourage high achievement by our young people and to provide benchmarks to determine how well they are learning and performing. In 1992, anticipating that education standards would emerge as a focal point of the reform legislation, the Consortium of National Arts Education Associations successfully approached the U.S. Department of Education, the National Endowment for the Arts, and the National Endowment for the Humanities for a grant to determine what the nation's school children should know and be able to do in the arts. This document is the result of an extended process of consensus-building that drew on the broadest possible range of expertise and participation. The process involved the review of state-level arts education frameworks, standards from other nations, and consideration at a series of national forums.

The Importance of Standards

Agreement on what students should know and be able to do is essential if education is to be consistent, efficient, and effective. In this context, standards for arts education are important for two basic reasons. First, they help define what a good education in the arts should provide: a thorough grounding in a basic body of knowledge and the skills required both to make sense and make use of the arts disciplines. Second, when states and school districts adopt these standards, they are taking a stand for rigor in a part of education that has too often, and wrongly, been treated as optional. This document says, in effect, an education in the arts means that students should know what is spelled out here, and they should reach clear levels of attainment at these grade levels.

These standards provide a vision of competence and educational effectiveness, but without creating a mold into which all arts programs must fit. The standards are concerned with the results (in the form of student learning) that come from a basic education in the arts, not with how those results ought to be delivered. Those matters are for states, localities, and classroom teachers to decide. In other words, while the standards provide educational goals and not a curriculum, they can help improve all types of arts instruction.

The Importance of Arts Education

Knowing and practicing the arts disciplines are fundamental to the healthy development of children's minds and spirits. That is why, in any civilization—ours included—the arts are inseparable from the very meaning of the term education. We know from long experience that no one can claim to be truly educated who lacks basic knowledge and skills in the arts. There are many reasons for this assertion:

- The arts are worth studying simply because of what they are. Their impact cannot be denied. Throughout history, all the arts have served to connect our imaginations with the deepest questions of human existence: Who am I? What must I do? Where am I going? Studying responses to those questions through time and across cultures—as well as acquiring the tools and knowledge to create one's own responses—is essential not only to understanding life but to living it fully.
- The arts are used to achieve a multitude of human purposes: to present issues and ideas, to teach or persuade, to entertain, to decorate or please. Becoming literate in the arts helps students understand and do these things better.
- The arts are integral to every person's daily life. Our personal, social, economic, and cultural environments are shaped by the arts at every turn—from the design of the child's breakfast placemat, to the songs on the commuter's car radio, to the family's nighttime TV drama, to the teenager's Saturday dance, to the enduring influences of the classics.

- The arts offer unique sources of enjoyment and refreshment for the imagination. They explore relationships between ideas and objects and serve as links between thought and action. Their continuing gift is to help us see and grasp life in new ways.
- There is ample evidence that the arts help students develop the attitudes, characteristics, and intellectual skills required to participate effectively in today's society and economy. The arts teach self-discipline, reinforce self-esteem, and foster the thinking skills and creativity so valued in the workplace. They teach the importance of teamwork and cooperation. They demonstrate the direct connection between study, hard work, and high levels of achievement.

The Benefits of Arts Education

Arts education benefits the student because it cultivates the whole child, gradually building many kinds of literacy while developing intuition, reasoning, imagination, and dexterity into unique forms of expression and communication. This process requires not merely an active mind but a trained one. An education in the arts benefits society because students of the arts gain powerful tools for understanding human experiences, both past and present. They learn to respect the often very different ways others have of thinking, working, and expressing themselves. They learn to make decisions in situations where there are no standard answers. By studying the arts, students stimulate their natural creativity and learn to develop it to meet the needs of a complex and competitive society. And, as study and competence in the arts reinforce one other, the joy of learning becomes real, tangible, and powerful.

The Arts and Other Core Subjects

The standards address competence in the arts disciplines first of all. But that competence provides a firm foundation for connecting arts-related concepts and facts across the art forms, and from them to the sciences and humanities. For example, the intellectual methods of the arts are precisely those used to transform scientific disciplines and discoveries into everyday technology.

What Must We Do?

The educational success of our children depends on creating a society that is both literate and imaginative, both competent and creative. That goal depends, in turn, on providing children with tools not only for understanding that world but for contributing to it and making their own way. Without the arts to help shape student's perceptions and imaginations, our children stand every chance of growing into adulthood as culturally disabled. We must not allow that to happen.

Without question, the standards presented here will need supporters and allies to improve how arts education is organized and delivered. They have the potential to change education policy at all levels, and to make a transforming impact across the entire spectrum of education.

But only if they are implemented.

Teachers, of course, will be the leaders in this process. In many places, more teachers with credentials in the arts, as well as better-trained teachers in general, will be needed. Site-based management teams, school boards, state education agencies, state and local arts agencies, and teacher education institutions will all have a part to play, as will local mentors, artists, local arts organizations, and members of the community. Their support is crucial for the standards to succeed. But the primary issue is the ability to bring together and deliver a broad range of competent instruction. All else is secondary.

In the end, truly successful implementation can come about only when students and their learning are at the center, which means motivating and enabling them to meet the standards. With a steady gaze on that target, these standards can empower America's schools to make changes consistent with the best any of us can envision, for our children and for our society.

NATIONAL STANDARDS FOR MUSIC EDUCATION

1. Singing, alone and with others, a varied repertoire of music.
2. Performing on instruments, alone and with others, a varied repertoire of music.
3. Improvising melodies, variations, and accompaniments.

4. Composing and arranging music within specified guidelines.
5. Reading and notating music.
6. Listening to, analyzing, and describing music.
7. Evaluating music and music performances.
8. Understanding relationships between music, the other arts, and disciplines outside the arts.
9. Understanding music in relation to history and culture.

Appendix G

Where We Stand: A Position Paper of the Music Educators National Conference, 1997

This statement clarified MENC's position on such topics as the role of music in American education, conditions and expectations for music instruction, and current issues in music education. A number of professional organizations endorsed and supported these positions. Adopted by the MENC National Executive Board, March 1997.

The Music Educators National Conference is the only national professional organization that addresses all aspects of music education. Its more than 70,000 members represent all levels of teaching from preschool to graduate school. Since 1907, MENC has worked to improve the lives of America's young people by promoting access to a balanced, comprehensive, and high-quality program of music instruction taught by certified and qualified teachers. The following statements represent MENC's position on a variety of topics and issues that concern music education.

THE ROLE OF MUSIC IN AMERICAN EDUCATION

Music and the Other Basics

1. The Arts constitute one of the five fundamental components of basic education, along with language arts, mathematics, physical sciences,

and social sciences. These fields of study should be at the core of every child's education.

2. The Arts are defined as music, visual arts, theatre, and dance. Only courses that emphasize these subjects should be accepted as satisfying requirements in the visual and performing arts.

3. Every high school should require at least one year of study in music, visual arts, theatre, or dance for graduation and should encourage additional study in the arts.

4. Every college and university should require at least one year of study in music, visual arts, theatre, or dance for admission and should encourage additional study in the arts.

Access to Music Education

1. Because of the role of the arts in civilization, and because of their unique ability to communicate the ideas and emotions of the human spirit, every American student, preK through grade 12, should receive a balanced, comprehensive, sequential, and rigorous program of instruction in music and the other arts. This includes students in public schools, private schools, and charter schools, as well as home-schooled students.

2. Music study should be a required part of education for every student each year through grade 8, and every student in grades 9–12 should have the opportunity to elect music study each year.

Support for Music Education

1. The professional staff of every state education agency should include a music supervisor, coordinator, or specialist in order to provide professional leadership and assistance to local boards of education, teachers, and administrators, as well as to facilitate liaison with local communities and decision makers.

2. Every school or school system should provide adequate financial resources to support a quality music program as described in *Opportunity-to-Learn Standards for Music Instruction*. In public schools, this support should come from public funds. Programs should not be dependent upon funds raised by students, teachers, or support groups.

3. If fiscal pressures require cutbacks in school programs, music should not suffer a cutback disproportionate to the rest of the instructional program. Cost reductions should be sought first by eliminating auxiliary and noninstructional services. If further cutbacks are required, the goal should be to preserve a balanced curriculum at all grade levels as opposed to eliminating any part of the basic instructional program.
4. Preservice and in-service education for teaching music should be designed to help music educators plan and teach a comprehensive music program based on the National Standards for Music Education.

Objectives of Music Education

1. The music program should be based on the skills and knowledge outlined in The School Music Program: A New Vision. These skills and knowledge will provide students with a well-grounded understanding of the nature, value, and meaning of music in order that they may participate fully in their musical culture.
2. The preK music education program should enable children to explore music by:
   • singing and playing instruments
   • creating music
   • responding to music
   • understanding music

   The K–12 music program should enable students to develop skills and knowledge in:

   • singing, alone and with others, a varied repertoire of music
   • performing on instruments, alone and with others, a varied repertoire of music
   • improvising melodies, variations, and accompaniments
   • composing and arranging music within specified guidelines
   • reading and notating music
   • listening to, analyzing, and describing music
   • evaluating music and music performances
   • understanding relationships between music, the other arts, and disciplines outside the arts
   • understanding music in relation to history and culture

CONDITIONS AND EXPECTATIONS FOR MUSIC EDUCATION

The Importance of Standards for Music Instruction

1. Both history and practice support the belief that there is a high correlation between successful student learning in music and the existence of favorable learning conditions. Detailed standards for curriculum and scheduling, staffing, materials and equipment, and facilities necessary to implement the program described in The School Music Program: A New Vision are described in Opportunity-to-Learn Standards for Music Instruction.

Curriculum and Scheduling

1. The music curriculum should (1) be suited to the needs of the individual students, (2) reflect the multicultural nature of our pluralistic American culture, (3) include music of the world and other times in history, (4) be responsive to the requirements of the diverse populations in our schools, including the musically talented, (5) provide sufficient course offerings for students to participate in performance and nonperformance courses, and (6) incorporate the media and technology of contemporary America.
2. The music curriculum should be described and outlined in a series of sequential curriculum guides for each grade level or course offering.
3. Music should be taught during the school day.
   - Every elementary school student should receive at least ninety minutes of general music instruction each week in periods of age-appropriate length.
   - Alternative scheduling initiatives, such as block scheduling, multiage grouping, and year-round schools, should provide every student with the same access to comprehensive, balanced, and sequential music instruction as more traditional scheduling procedures. In schools with traditional schedules, the school day should include no fewer than eight instructional periods.
4. All secondary school programs should include course offerings in instrumental, choral, and general music.

5. Opportunities to begin instrumental music instruction should be available at all levels beginning no later than the upper elementary level as outlined in *Opportunity-to-Learn Standards for Music Instruction.*

6. The study of music should be integrated as appropriate into all of the disciplines of the curriculum. Similarly, content from other disciplines can be used effectively to enrich the study of music. In efforts to integrate instruction, the study of music should maintain its integrity and music should be taught primarily for its own sake rather than as a means to achieve nonmusical goals.

Staffing

All levels:

1. Music should be taught by certified and qualified teachers. The contributions of professional musicians and classroom teachers may complement but not substitute for a balanced, comprehensive, and sequential music program taught primarily by certified and qualified teachers.

2. In order that the instructional program be adequately coordinated and articulated from level to level, one or more music educators, according to the size of the district, should be designated as coordinator, supervisor, or administrator and appropriately compensated and supported.

3. Professional development opportunities should be provided for all music educators to increase their musical knowledge and skills, to learn new instructional strategies and to remain current in the profession.

4. Every music educator should have at least thirty minutes during each school day for preparation, planning, and student evaluation.

5. Sufficient travel time should be calculated in the teaching schedule of every music educator who must move from school to school or room to room.

6. Students with disabilities should, to the fullest extent possible, have the opportunity to participate in elective choral and instrumental

experiences. Teacher aides or paraprofessionals should be provided in music classes for students who require them in other classes.

Elementary:

1. In the elementary grades, classroom teachers should be qualified to complement the music instruction delivered by the music specialist.
2. The music teacher:student ratio should be no higher than 1:400.

Secondary:

1. An accompanist should be provided during regular daily rehearsals for choral ensemble classes.

Materials and Equipment

1. Every teacher should be provided with sufficient and appropriate materials, instruments, and equipment with which to teach. All materials should be current and in good condition. All equipment should be of high quality and in good repair.
2. Every student should have access to appropriate educational technology and the opportunity to explore its potential. Technology should be used to achieve the objectives of music education, rather than used for its own sake.
3. An annual budget should be provided to update materials and equipment and for the repair or replacement of equipment necessary for music instruction.

Facilities

1. Every music educator should be provided with appropriate facilities in which to teach and plan. All facilities should be large enough to accommodate the largest group taught.
2. All facilities should have adequate acoustical properties and should provide sufficient, secured storage. Additionally, music programs

should have access to a performance facility with acoustical properties to appropriately showcase student performance.

CURRENT ISSUES IN MUSIC EDUCATION

Academic Eligibility Requirements

Academic eligibility requirements are not appropriate when applied to students enrolled in scheduled, credit-bearing music classes, including performance groups. Such classes include requirements for out-of-school performances, concerts, festivals, and other activities that serve as laboratories to demonstrate and assess what has been learned.

Supplementary Fees

No student should be required to pay a supplementary fee to participate in a scheduled, credit-bearing music class.

Music with Religious Texts

The study and performance of music with religious texts within an educational context is a vital and appropriate part of a comprehensive music education. The omission of sacred music from the school curriculum would result in an incomplete educational experience. Music educators should demonstrate sensitivity to the diversity of beliefs represented by their students.

Assessment of Students, Teachers, and Programs

Every school district should use reliable, valid, and appropriate instruments and techniques for assessing student learning, teacher competence, and program effectiveness in music. Music educators should be effectively represented on the committees that establish the criteria, materials, and procedures by which music educators are evaluated. Special instruments, items, or techniques may be required to evaluate the special competencies needed by music educators. The evaluator of a music educator, or at least one member of the evaluation team, should be knowledgeable about music education.

Magnet Schools

Magnet schools can provide an enriched music education for musically talented or interested students. Such schools may play an important part in the music instruction program of a school district provided they do not result in a reduction in the quantity or quality of music instruction in other schools within the district.

Travel

Trips by school music organizations should be justified on the basis of their educational value to students. Teachers should consider the following in making decisions regarding whether or not to schedule a trip: (1) the effect of the trip on the students' educational programs, (2) the cost and effort required in relation to the educational value, (3) the age of the students, and (4) the effect of the trip on other aspects of the music curriculum and the total school curriculum.

Educational Partnerships

Music educators should seek opportunities to advance music education by utilizing the resources of their communities and by working cooperatively with other individuals and groups such as professional musicians, the music industry, arts organizations, and educational organizations.

The Music Code of Ethics

In making judgments concerning the jurisdictions of professional musicians and school musicians, music educators should be guided by The Music Code of Ethics, an agreement signed by the American Federation of Musicians, MENC, the American Association of School Administrators, the National Association of Elementary School Principals, and the National Association of Secondary School Principals.

RESOURCES

"The Music Code of Ethics." Reston, VA: Music Educators National Conference, 1997.

Opportunity-to-Learn Standards for Music Instruction: Grades PreK–12. Reston, VA: Music Educators National Conference, 1994.

Performance Standards for Music: Strategies and Benchmarks for Assessing Progress toward the National Standards—Grades PreK–12. Reston, VA: Music Educators National Conference, 1996.

"Religious Music in the Schools." Reston, VA: Music Educators National Conference, 1996.

The School Music Program: A New Vision. The K–12 National Standards, PreK Standards, and What They Mean to Music Educators. Reston, VA: Music Educators National Conference, 1994.

ENDORSERS

The following professional organizations join with MENC in promoting this music education position paper:

American Association of School Administrators
American Bandmasters Association
American Federation of Musicians
American Music Conference
American String Teachers Association
American Symphony Orchestra League
BMI
Chamber Music America
Council for Basic Education
Fender Musical Instruments
Future Business Leaders of America
National Association of College Wind and Percussion Instructors
National Association of Pastoral Musicians
National Association of School Music Dealers
National Federation of Music Clubs
National Piano Foundation
National School Orchestra Association

Piano Manufacturers Association International
SPEBSQSA, Inc.
Sweet Adelines International

SUPPORTERS

The following professional organizations have added their support for the goals and ideals implied in the music education position paper:

American Guild of English Handbell Ringers
Association of Teacher Educators
National Assembly of State Arts Agencies
National Association of Schools of Art and Design
National Association of Schools of Dance
National Association of Schools of Music
National Association of Schools of Theatre
National Association of Secondary School Principals
National Guild of Community Schools of the Arts
Young Audiences, Inc.

Adopted by the National Executive Board, March 1997
MENC: The National Association for Music Education
1806 Robert Fulton Drive
Reston, VA 20191

Appendix H

The Value and Quality of Arts Education: A Statement of Principles, 1999

A statement on the importance of arts education, developed by the Consortium of Arts Education Associations and signed by major stakeholders in education.

We, the undersigned representatives of professional education associations, share a deep concern about the nature, role, importance, and future of arts education in the schools where our members teach, administer, supervise, and make and implement education policy.

We are unanimous in our agreement that all Americans who share our concern about the quality of education in general, and of arts education in particular (dance, visual arts, music, theatre), should understand the value of arts education for every child, and we encourage those who will work with us to enhance and support arts education in our nation's schools. To that end, we invite all Americans, both within the professional education community and outside it, to join us in support of the following principles.

First, every student in the nation should have an education in the arts.

This means that all PreK–12 students must have a comprehensive, balanced, sequential, in-school program of instruction in the arts, taught by qualified teachers, designed to provide students of all ages with skills and knowledge in the arts in accordance with high national, state, and local standards.

Can be found at www.menc.org/about/view/menc-position-statements.

Second, to ensure a basic education in the arts for all students, the arts should be recognized as serious, core academic subjects.

The arts should not be treated as extracurricular activities, but as integral core disciplines. In practice, this means that effective arts education requires sequential curricula, regular time-on-task, qualified teachers, and a fair share of educational resources. Similarly, arts instruction should be carried out with the same academic rigor and high expectations as instruction in other core subjects.

Third, as education policy makers make decisions, they should incorporate the multiple lessons of recent research concerning the value and impact of arts education.

The arts have a unique ability to communicate the ideas and emotions of the human spirit. Connecting us to our history, our traditions, and our heritage, the arts have a beauty and power unique in our culture. At the same time, a growing body of research indicates that education in the arts provides significant cognitive benefits and bolsters academic achievement, beginning at an early age and continuing through school. (See appendix for supporting examples.)

Fourth, qualified arts teachers and sequential curriculum must be recognized as the basis and core for substantive arts education for all students.

Teachers who are qualified as arts educators by virtue of academic study and artistic practice provide the very best arts education possible. In-school arts programs are designed to reach and teach all students, not merely the interested, the talented, or those with a particular socioeconomic background. These teachers and curricula should be supported by local school budgets and tax dollars, nurtured by higher education, and derive direct professional development benefits from outstanding teachers and trainers in the organizations we represent. Several national education associations identify the arts as essential learning in which students must demonstrate achievement. (Breaking Ranks, NASSP, 1996; *Principal* magazine, NAESP, March, 1998.)

Fifth, arts education programs should be grounded in rigorous instruction, provide meaningful assessment of academic progress and performance, and take their place within a structure of direct accountability to school officials, parents, and the community.

In-school programs that are fully integrated into state and local curricula afford the best potential for achieving these ends.

Sixth, community resources that provide exposure to the arts, enrichment, and entertainment through the arts all offer valuable support and enhancement to an in-school arts education.

As a matter of policy or practice, however, these kinds of activities cannot substitute for a comprehensive, balanced, sequential arts education taught by qualified teachers, as shaped by clear standards and focused by the content of the arts disciplines.

Seventh, and finally, we offer our unified support to those programs, policies, and practitioners that reflect these principles.

On behalf of the students we teach, the schools we administer and work in, and the communities we serve, we ask all Americans who care deeply about making the whole spectrum of cultural and cognitive development available to their children to join us in protecting and advancing opportunities for all children to receive an education in the arts.

American Association of School Administrators

With 15,000 members, the American Association of School Administrators, founded in 1865, is a professional organization for superintendents, central office administrators, and other system-wide leaders.

American Federation of Teachers

The American Federation of Teachers, which has more than 2,100 locals nationwide and a 1998 membership of 980,000, was founded in 1916 to represent the economic, social, and professional interests of classroom teachers.

Association for Supervision and Curriculum Development

The Association for Supervision and Curriculum Development is an international, nonprofit, nonpartisan education association committed to the mission of forging covenants in teaching and learning for the success of all learners. ASCD was founded in 1943 and is one of the largest professional education associations in the world, with membership approaching 200,000.

Council for Basic Education

The mission of the Council for Basic Education is to strengthen teaching and learning of the basic subjects—English, history, government, geography, mathematics, the sciences, foreign languages, and the arts. CBE, with a readership base of 3,000, advocates high academic standards and the promotion of a strong liberal arts education for all children in the nation's elementary and secondary schools.

Council of Chief State School Officers

The Council of Chief State School Officers represents public officials who lead the departments responsible for elementary and secondary education in the states. CCSSO advocates legislative positions of the members and assists state agencies with their leadership capacity.

National Association of Elementary School Principals

Dedicated to educational excellence and high professional standards among K–8 educators, the National Association of Elementary School Principals serves 28,000 elementary and middle school principals in the United States and abroad.

National Association of Secondary School Principals

The National Association of Secondary School Principals is the nation's largest organization of school administrators, representing 43,000 middle, junior, and senior high school principals and assistant principals. NASSP also administers the National Association of Student Activity Advisors, which represents 57,000 members, as well as the 22,000 chapters of the National Honor Society.

National Education Association

The National Education Association is the nation's largest professional employee organization, representing more than 2.4 million elementary and secondary teachers, higher education faculty, education support personnel, school administrators, retired educators, and students preparing to become teachers.

National Parent Teacher Association

The National PTA, representing 6.5 million members, is the largest volunteer child advocacy organization in the United States. An organization of parents, educators, students, and other citizens active in their schools and communities, the PTA is a leader in reminding our nation of its obligations to children. Membership in the National PTA is open to anyone who is concerned with the health, education, and welfare of children and youth.

National School Board Association

The National School Board Association represents the nation's 95,000 school board members through a federation of state associations and the school boards of the District of Columbia, Guam, Hawaii, and the U.S. Virgin Islands. NSBA's mission is to foster excellence and equity in public education through school board leadership.

APPENDIX

Supporting examples for Principle No. 3

There is a demonstrated, direct correlation between improved SAT scores and time spent studying the arts. In 1997, the College Board reported that students with four years of study in the arts outscored students with no arts instruction by a combined total of 101 points on the verbal and mathematics portions of the SAT.

Statistically significant links are now being reported between music instruction and tested intelligence in preschool children. In one widely cited study (Neurological Research, Feb. 1997), after six months, students who had received keyboard instruction performed 34 percent higher on tests measuring temporal-spatial ability than did students without instruction. The findings indicate that music instruction enhances the same higher brain functions required for mathematics, chess, science, and engineering.

As numerous school-based programs have repeatedly reported around the country, study of the arts helps students think and integrate learning across traditional disciplinary lines. In the arts, they learn how to work cooperatively, pose and solve problems, and forge the vital link between individual (or group) effort and quality of result. These skills and attitudes, not incidentally, are vital for success in the twenty-first-century workplace. Sequential arts education also contributes to building technological competencies. It imparts academic discipline and teaches such higher level thinking skills as analyzing, synthesizing, and evaluating both personal experience and objective data. Finally, research findings indicate that arts education enhances students' respect for the cultures, belief systems, and values of their fellow learners.

MENC: The National Association for Music Education
1806 Robert Fulton Drive
Reston, Virginia 20191 (703) 860-4000
Publication Date: January 1999

Appendix I

"Vision 2020" Housewright Declaration, 1999

Summary of agreements made at the Housewright Symposium on the Future of Music Education, which updated the version for music education in the manner of the Tanglewood Symposium earlier.

THE HOUSEWRIGHT DECLARATION

Whenever and wherever humans have existed music has existed also. Since music occurs only when people choose to create and share it, and since they always have done so and no doubt always will, music clearly must have important value for people.

Music makes a difference in people's lives. It exalts the human spirit; it enhances the quality of life. Indeed, meaningful music activity should be experienced throughout one's life toward the goal of continuing involvement.

Music is a basic way of knowing and doing because of its own nature and because of the relationship of that nature to the human condition, including mind, body, and feeling. It is worth studying because it represents a basic mode of thought and action, and because in itself, it is one of the primary ways human beings create and share meanings. It must be studied fully to access this richness.

Clifford K. Madsen, ed., *Vision 2020: The Housewright Symposium on the Future of Music Education* (Reston, VA: MENC, 2000), 219–20. Also found at www.menc.org/resources/view/vision-2020-the-housewright-symposium-on-the-future-of-music-education.

Societal and technological changes will have an enormous impact for the future of music education. Changing demographics and increased technological advancements are inexorable and will have profound influences on the ways that music is experienced for both students and teachers.

Music educators must build on the strengths of current practice to take responsibility for charting the future of music education to ensure that the best of the Western art tradition and other musical traditions are transmitted to future generations.

We agree on the following:

1. All persons, regardless of age, cultural heritage, ability, venue, or financial circumstance deserve to participate fully in the best music experiences possible.
2. The integrity of music study must be preserved. Music educators must lead the development of meaningful music instruction and experience.
3. Time must be allotted for formal music study at all levels of instruction such that a comprehensive, sequential, and standards-based program of music instruction is made available.
4. All music has a place in the curriculum. Not only does the Western art tradition need to be preserved and disseminated, music educators also need to be aware of other music that people experience and be able to integrate it into classroom music instruction.
5. Music educators need to be proficient and knowledgeable concerning technological changes and advancements and be prepared to use all appropriate tools in advancing music study while recognizing the importance of people coming together to make and share music.
6. Music educators should involve the music industry, other agencies, individuals, and music institutions in improving the quality and quantity of music instruction. This should start within each local community by defining the appropriate role of these resources in teaching and learning.
7. The currently defined role of the music educator will expand as settings for music instruction proliferate. Professional music educators must provide a leadership role in coordinating music activities beyond the school setting to ensure formal and informal curricular integration.

8. Recruiting prospective music teachers is a responsibility of many, including music educators. Potential teachers need to be drawn from diverse backgrounds, identified early, led to develop both teaching and musical abilities, and sustained through ongoing professional development. Also, alternative licensing should be explored in order to expand the number and variety of teachers available to those seeking music instruction.

9. Continuing research addressing all aspects of music activity needs to be supported including intellectual, emotional, and physical responses to music. Ancillary social results of music study also need exploration as well as specific studies to increase meaningful music listening.

10. Music making is an essential way in which learners come to know and understand music and music traditions. Music making should be broadly interpreted to be performing, composing, improvising, listening, and interpreting music notation.

11. Music educators must join with others in providing opportunities for meaningful music instruction for all people beginning at the earliest possible age and continuing throughout life.

12. Music educators must identify the barriers that impede the full actualization of any of the above and work to overcome them.

Appendix J

No Child Left Behind Act of 2001 Definitions

In definitions of Section 9101, "arts" are listed among other "core academic subjects."

An act to close the achievement gap with accountability, flexibility, and choice so that no child is left behind.

Be it enacted by the Senate and House of Representatives of the United States of America in Congress assembled.

SECTION 1. SHORT TITLE

This title may be cited as the "No Child Left Behind Act of 2001."

SECTION 2. TABLE OF CONTENTS

The table of contents for this Act is as follows:

Sec. 1. Short title.
Sec. 2. Table of contents.
Sec. 3. References.
Sec. 4. Transition.

No Child Left Behind Act of 2001, Public Law 107-110, *U.S. Statutes at Large* 115 (2002): 1425, 1956–58. Also available at www.ed.gov/policy/elsec/leg/esea02/pg107.html#sec9101.

Sec. 5. Effective date.

Sec. 6. Table of contents of Elementary and Secondary Education Act of 1965.

Title I—Improving the Academic Achievement of the Disadvantaged

Sec. 101. Improving the academic achievement of the disadvantaged.

Title II—Preparing, Training, and Recruiting High Quality Teachers and Principals

Sec. 201. Teacher and principal training and recruiting fund.

Sec. 202. Continuation of awards.

Title III—Language Instruction for Limited English Proficient and Immigrant Students

Sec. 301. Language instruction for limited English proficient children and immigrant children and youth.

Title IV—21st Century Schools

Sec. 401. 21st Century schools.

Title V—Promoting Informed Parental Choice and Innovative Programs

Sec. 501. Innovative programs and parental choice provisions.

Sec. 502. Continuation of awards.

Title VI—Flexibility and Accountability

Sec. 601. Flexibility and accountability.

Sec. 602. Amendment to the National Education Statistics Act of 1994.

Title VII—Indian, Native Hawaiian, and Alaska Native Education

Sec. 701. Indians, Native Hawaiians, and Alaska Natives.

Sec. 702. Conforming amendments.

Sec. 703. Savings provisions.

Title VIII—Impact Aid Program

Sec. 801. Payments relating to Federal acquisition of real property.

"(ii) the Committee on Appropriations and the Committee on Health, Education, Labor, and Pensions of the Senate."

SEC. 804. STATE CONSIDERATION OF PAYMENTS IN PROVIDING STATE AID

Section 8009(b)(1) (20 U.S.C. 7709(b)(1)) is amended by inserting after "section 8003(a)(2)(B)" the following: "and, with respect to a local educational agency that receives a payment under section 8003(b)(2), the amount in excess of the amount that the agency would receive if the agency were deemed to be an agency eligible to receive a payment under section 8003(b)(1) and not section 8003(b)(2)."

SEC. 805. AUTHORIZATION OF APPROPRIATIONS

(a) In General.—Section 8014 (20 U.S.C. 7714) is amended in subsections (a), (b), (c), and (f) by striking "three succeeding fiscal years" each place it appears and inserting "seven succeeding fiscal years."

(b) Construction.—Section 8014(e) (20 U.S.C. 7714(e)) is amended by striking "for each of the three succeeding fiscal years" and inserting "for fiscal year 2001, $150,000,000 for fiscal year 2002, and such sums as may be necessary for each of the five succeeding fiscal years."

(c) Additional assistance for certain local educational agencies impacted by federal property acquisition.—Section 8014 (20 U.S.C. 7714) is amended by striking subsection (g).

TITLE IX—GENERAL PROVISIONS

Sec. 901. General Provisions.

Title IX (20 U.S.C. 7801 et seq.) is amended to read as follows:

Title IX—General Provisions
Part A—Definitions
20 USN 7801 Sec. 9101. Definitions.

Except as otherwise provided, in this Act:

(1) Average Daily Attendance—

    (A) In General—Except as provided otherwise by State law or this paragraph, the term "average daily attendance" means—"(i) the aggregate number of days of attendance of all students during a school year; divided by (ii) the number of days school is in session during that year."

    (B) Conversion—The Secretary shall permit the conversion of average daily membership (or other similar data) to average daily attendance for local educational agencies in States that provide State aid to local educational agencies on the basis of average daily membership (or other similar data).

    (C) Special Rule—If the local educational agency in which a child resides makes a tuition or other payment for the free public education of the child in a school located in another school district, the Secretary shall, for the purpose of this Act—"(i) consider the child to be in attendance at a school of the agency making the payment; and (ii) not consider the child to be in attendance at a school of the agency receiving the payment."

    (D) Children with Disabilities—If a local educational agency makes a tuition payment to a private school or to a public school of another local educational agency for a child with a disability, as defined in section 602 of the Individuals with Disabilities Education Act, the Secretary shall, for the purpose of this Act, consider the child to be in attendance at a school of the agency making the payment.

(2) Average Per-Pupil Expenditure—The term "average per-pupil expenditure" means, in the case of a State or of the United States—

    (A) without regard to the source of funds—"(i) the aggregate current expenditures, during the third fiscal year preceding the fiscal year for which the determination is made (or, if satisfactory data for that year are not available, during the most recent preceding fiscal year for which satisfactory data are available) of all local educational agencies in the State or, in the case of the United States, for all States (which, for the purpose of this paragraph, means the 50 States and the District of Columbia); plus (ii) any direct current expenditures by the State for the operation of those agencies; divided by

(B) the aggregate number of children in average daily attendance to whom those agencies provided free public education during that preceding year.

(3) Beginning Teacher—The term "beginning teacher" means a teacher in a public school who has been teaching less than a total of three complete school years.

(4) Child—The term "child" means any person within the age limits for which the State provides free public education.

(5) Child with a Disability—The term "child with a disability" has the same meaning given that term in section 602 of the Individuals with Disabilities Education Act.

(6) Community-Based Organization—The term "community-based organization" means a public or private nonprofit organization of demonstrated effectiveness that—

(A) is representative of a community or significant segments of a community; and

(B) provides educational or related services to individuals in the community.

(7) Consolidated Local Application—The term "consolidated local application" means an application submitted by a local educational agency pursuant to section 9305.

(8) Consolidated Local Plan—The term "consolidated local plan" means a plan submitted by a local educational agency pursuant to section 9305.

(9) Consolidated State Application—The term "consolidated State application" means an application submitted by a State educational agency pursuant to section 9302.

(10) Consolidated State Plan—The term "consolidated State plan" means a plan submitted by a State educational agency pursuant to section 9302.

(11) **Core Academic Subjects—The term "core academic subjects" means English, reading or language arts, mathematics, science, foreign languages, civics and government, economics, arts, history, and geography.**

(12) County—The term "county" means one of the divisions of a State used by the Secretary of Commerce in compiling and reporting data regarding counties.

(13) Covered Program—The term "covered program" means each of the programs authorized by—

(A) part A of title I;

(B) subpart 3 of part B of title I;

(C) part C of title I;

(D) part D of title I;

(E) part F of title I;

(F) part A of title II;

(G) part D of title II;

(H) part A of title III;

(I) part A of title IV;

(J) part B of title IV;

(K) part A of title V; and

(L) subpart 2 of part B of title VI.

(14) Current Expenditures—The term "current expenditures" means expenditures for free public education—

(A) including expenditures for administration, instruction, attendance and health services, pupil transportation services, operation and maintenance of plant, fixed charges, and net expenditures to cover deficits for food services and student body activities; but

(B) not including expenditures for community services, capital outlay, and debt service, or any expenditures made from funds received under title I and part A of title V.

(15) Department—The term "Department" means the Department of Education.

(16) Distance Learning—The term "distance learning" means the transmission of educational or instructional programming to geographically dispersed individuals and groups via telecommunications.

(17) Educational Service Agency—The term "educational service agency" means a regional public multiservice agency authorized by State statute to develop, manage, and provide services or programs to local educational agencies.

(18) Elementary School—The term "elementary school" means a non-profit institutional day or residential school, including a public elementary charter school, that provides elementary education, as determined under State law.

(19) Exemplary Teacher—The term "exemplary teacher" means a teacher who—

   (A) is a highly qualified teacher such as a master teacher;

   (B) has been teaching for at least 5 years in a public or private school or institution of higher education;

   (C) is recommended to be an exemplary teacher by administrators and other teachers who are knowledgeable about the individual's performance;

Appendix K

A Policy Letter on the Arts from Former Secretary of Education Rod Paige, 2004

In a letter addressed to education superintendents, Rod Paige sets the record straight about interpretation of the role of arts programs in the curriculum.

KEY POLICY LETTERS SIGNED BY THE EDUCATION SECRETARY OR DEPUTY SECRETARY, JULY 2004

Dear Superintendent:

As I am sure you know, the arts are a core academic subject under the No Child Left Behind Act (NCLB). I believe the arts have a significant role in education both for their intrinsic value and for the ways in which they can enhance general academic achievement and improve students' social and emotional development.

As I travel the country, I often hear that arts education programs are endangered because of No Child Left Behind. This message was echoed in a recent series of teacher roundtables sponsored by the Department of Education. It is both disturbing and just plain wrong.

It's disturbing not just because arts programs are being diminished or eliminated, but because NCLB is being interpreted so narrowly as to be

---

Available at www.ed.gov/policy/elsec/guid/secletter/040701.html.

considered the reason for these actions. The truth is that NCLB included the arts as a core academic subject because of their importance to a child's education. No Child Left Behind expects teachers of the arts to be highly qualified, just as it does teachers of English, math, science, and history.

The Value of the Arts

The arts, perhaps more than any other subject, help students to understand themselves and others, whether they lived in the past or are living in the present. President Bush recognizes this important contribution of the arts to every child's education. He has said, "From music and dance to painting and sculpting, the arts allow us to explore new worlds and to view life from another perspective." In addition, they "encourage individuals to sharpen their skills and abilities and to nurture their imagination and intellect."

A comprehensive arts education may encompass such areas as the history of the arts, the honing of critical analysis skills, the re-creation of classic as well as contemporary works of art, and the expression of students' ideas and feelings through the creation of their own works of art. In other words, students should have the opportunity to respond to, perform, and create in the arts.

Setting the Record Straight

There is much flexibility for states and local school districts under the No Child Left Behind Act with respect to support for the core subjects. In Arizona, for example, as part of Superintendent Tom Horne's current "content-rich curriculum" initiative, $4 million in Comprehensive School Reform (Title I, Part F) funds are supporting arts education at 43 current Comprehensive School Reform schools throughout the state. Additional Arizona Arts Education Initiative school sites are being supported with Title V (Innovative Programs) funding under NCLB.

Under NCLB, Title I, Part A funds also can be used by local education agencies to improve the educational achievement of disadvantaged students through the arts. In the same way, Title II Teacher Quality Enhancement Grants can address the professional development needs of teachers of the arts, and portions of Title II funds can support partnerships that include nonprofit, cultural-arts organizations.

The arts also can be an important part of learning and enrichment in programs supported by 21st Century Community Learning Centers program funds. Before- and after-school, weekend, and summer programs are excellent opportunities to stimulate students' artistic interests and foster their growth or to integrate arts learning with other subjects, including reading and math. Cultural partners in the community—arts centers, symphonies, theatres, and the like—can offer engaging venues as well as skilled instructors and mentors for students.

Various information about some of the publications available on arts education is enclosed. We are providing this information for your convenience, and you may want to share these resources with your state department or central office staff as well as with your administrators, principals, and teachers.

The Value-Added Benefits of the Arts

In keeping with NCLB's principle of classroom practices based on research evidence, studies have shown that arts teaching and learning can increase students' cognitive and social development. The arts can be a critical link for students in developing the crucial thinking skills and motivations they need to achieve at higher levels. *Critical Links: Learning in the Arts and Student Academic and Social Development*, a research compendium of the Arts Education Partnership, offers evidence of such links, including connections between arts learning and achievement in reading and math.

Based on a review of data from the National Educational Longitudinal Study (NELS: 88), University of California–Los Angeles researchers determined that students who were highly involved in arts instruction earned better grades and performed better on standardized tests. They also performed more community service, watched fewer hours of television, reported less boredom in school, and were less likely to drop out of school. These findings were also true for students from the lowest socioeconomic status quartile of the 25,000 students surveyed, belying the assumption that socioeconomic status, rather than arts engagement, contributes to such gains in academic achievement and social involvement. As mentioned in the enclosure, a summary of these and other findings in *Critical Links* can be accessed at the Arts Education Partnership's Web site at: www.aep-arts.org/resources/toolkits/criticallinks/.

For both the important knowledge and skills they impart and the ways in which they help students to succeed in school and in life, the arts are an important part of a complete education. As we work together to implement NCLB, let's ensure that all children have the opportunity to learn and to grow in and through the arts.

Sincerely,
Rod Paige

Appendix L

Resolution in Recognition of Music Education, 2007

Resolution introduced in the U.S. Senate by Senator Chris Dodd (D-CT) and Senator Lamar Alexander (R-TN), members of the Senate Committee on Health, Education, Labor and Pensions. They also sent a letter requesting that the Government Accountability Office conduct a study on access to music and arts education in the American public school system since passage of the No Child Left Behind Act of 2001. This is the most recent of many such resolutions supporting education in music and the other arts.

RECOGNIZING THE BENEFITS AND IMPORTANCE OF SCHOOL-BASED MUSIC EDUCATION IN THE SENATE OF THE UNITED STATES

Mr. Alexander (for himself and Mr. Dodd) submitted the following concurrent resolution;

Concurrent Resolution

Recognizing the benefits and importance of school-based music education.

Whereas school music programs enhance intellectual development and enrich the academic environment for students of all ages;

Available at http://dodd.senate.gov/multimedia/2007/050807_Music.pdf.

Whereas students who participate in school music programs are less likely to be involved with drugs, gangs, or alcohol, and have better attendance in school;

Whereas the skills gained through sequential music instruction, including discipline and the ability to analyze, solve problems, communicate, and work cooperatively, are vital for success in the twenty-first-century workplace;

Whereas the majority of students attending public schools in inner city neighborhoods have virtually no access to music education, which places them at a disadvantage compared to their peers in other communities;

Whereas the arts are a core academic subject, and music is an essential element of the arts; and

Whereas every student in the United States should have an opportunity to reap the benefits of music education: Now, therefore, be it *Resolved by the Senate (the House of Representatives concurring)*, that it is the sense of the Congress that music education grounded in rigorous instruction is an important component of a well-rounded academic curriculum and should be available to every student in every school in the United States.

DODD, ALEXANDER CALL FOR
STUDY OF ACCESS TO ARTS EDUCATION

Introduce Resolution in Recognition of Music Education, May 8, 2007

Today Senator Chris Dodd (D-CT) and Senator Lamar Alexander (R-TN) sent a letter to David Walker, the comptroller general of the Government Accountability Office (GAO), requesting that the GAO conduct a study on access to music and arts education in the American public school system since passage of the No Child Left Behind Act. This week, Senators Dodd and Alexander also introduced a resolution recognizing the benefits and importance of school-based music education. Senators Dodd and Alexander are members of the Senate Committee on Health, Education, Labor and Pensions (HELP), and are chairman and ranking member of its Subcommittee on Children and Families.

"No child should be deprived of the chance to explore his or her creativity in a nurturing educational environment," said Dodd. "Picking up a musical instrument, a paint brush, or a script can allow a child to discover a hidden talent and can serve as a much-needed positive influence in the midst of the many difficult decisions that young people face today. I am hopeful that the GAO will act quickly to deliver findings about the current condition of arts education in American public schools so that we can seek to improve it during the reauthorization of the No Child Left Behind Act."

Added Alexander: "Music Education is important. I had some great teachers, but my piano teacher, Miss Lennis Tedford was the best. From age five until my high school senior recital, I spent thirty minutes with her each week. 'Don't play that monkey business,' she would say, as she could always tell when I'd been playing too much Jerry Lee Lewis. From Miss Tedford I learned more than music. She taught me the discipline of Czerny and the metronome, the logic of Bach, the clean joy of Mozart. She encouraged me to let my emotions run with Chopin and Rachmaninoff. She made sure I was ready for the annual piano competition, and that I performed completely under control. I still thank her for the discipline and love of music she gave me each time I sit at the piano today."

A companion resolution—introduced by Reps. Jim Cooper (D-TN) and Jon Porter (R-NV)—passed the House of Representatives on April 26 by unanimous consent.

The full text of the letter is below:

The Honorable David M. Walker
Comptroller General
Government Accountability Office
441 G Street N.W.
Washington, DC 20548

Dear Mr. Walker:

We write to request the Government Accountability Office to conduct a study on access to music and arts education in our public schools since passage of the No Child Left Behind Act, with a specific focus on any disparities in access between minority and low-income students and their non-minority, more affluent peers. The study should investigate evidence of the possible link between participation in music and arts education and increased student engagement, positive behavior, high school graduation rates and academic achievement for all students, as well as for minority and low-income students and students with disabilities.

As Congress moves toward reauthorization of the No Child Left Behind Act, we continue to examine the goals of educating the whole child and the positive impact of rigorous instruction in all areas of the curriculum. These policy decisions are based on sound research and driven by systematic data collection relating to the condition of education, the practices that improve academic achievement, and the effectiveness of federal education programs. Of particular interest are the effects, since its implementation, of the No Child Left Behind Act on access to music and arts education in our nation's public schools.

Specifically, we request the Government Accountability Office to design and implement a study that determines the following with regard to K–12 academic instruction in our public schools.

- Any changes in access to music and arts education since passage of the No Child Left Behind Act.
- Access to music and arts education for minority students relative to non-minority students.
- Access to music and arts education for low-income students relative to non–low income students.
- Any disparities in access to music and arts education, since passage of the No Child Left Behind Act, between schools with high percentages of minority and low-income students and students with disabilities and those schools with low percentages of such students.
- Any link between participation in music and arts education and increased student engagement, positive behavior, high school graduation and academic achievement for all students, as well as any such link for minority and low-income students and students with disabilities.
- Descriptions of highly effective music and arts education programs that promote increased student engagement, positive behavior, high school graduation and academic achievement.
- Identification of any barriers actively imposed by Federal law, regulations, or guidance that prevent schools from engaging students in a rich curriculum that includes music and arts.

Because consideration of the No Child Left Behind Act reauthorization has already begun, the need for this information is immediate. We request that you meet with representatives of our offices as soon as possible to discuss the proposed scope of this study, an appropriate methodology, and a timetable which would establish an interim reporting schedule and completion date.

We look forward to hearing from you regarding this request and your availability to meet as soon as possible to set forth plans for receipt of this information which will provide relevant insights into the impact of No Child Left Behind on access to music and arts education, especially for those students who have the fewest opportunities and greatest need.

Thank you for your assistance.

About the Contributors

Janet R. Barrett is associate professor of music education at the Bienen School of Music, Northwestern University. She served as president of the North Central Division of MENC from 2004 to 2006.

Anne L. Bryant is the executive director of the National School Boards Association, a federation of state and territorial organizations dedicated to advancing education through citizen governance of public schools.

Samuel Hope is executive director of the National Association of Schools of Music. He is the senior accreditation administrator in the United States and is known for his leadership in policy arenas. He serves as executive editor of the *Arts Education Policy Review*.

Former Arkansas Governor **Mike Huckabee** served from 1996 to 2007. In his role as chair of the Education Commission of the States, he championed arts education as the primary focus. He performs regularly with his band, Capitol Offense.

Paul Lehman is professor emeritus of music education at the University of Michigan. A past president of MENC, he has chaired groups responsible for crafting the National Standards in Music Education, served as chair of the Music Education Research Council, and as a member of the board of directors for the International Society for Music Education.

Michael Mark is professor emeritus of Towson University, where he also served as the dean of the graduate school. A noted historian in music education, Professor Mark is the author of numerous books, including a third edition of *A History of American Music Education* (2007).

Bennett Reimer is the John W. Beattie Professor of Music Emeritus at the Bienen School of Music, Northwestern University. He is the founder of the Center for the Study of Education and the Musical Experience and has authored or edited two dozen books and numerous articles on the philosophy of music education and other topics.

Brenda Lilienthal Welburn, chief executive officer of the National Association of State Boards of Education, has thirty years of experience in policy development and analysis in education and human services.